Praise for *CREATOR*

"If the path to enlightenment is paved with the gold of insight, then Steve Chandler's book, *CREATOR*, is the Yellow Brick Road. Every page, paragraph, and even line, it seems, resonates with the truth that is within me and awakens me to a desire to create. To progress. To Be."

~ **Andrew McKee,** author of *Change Your Game, Change Your Life*

***

"This is Steve Chandler's best book yet. His stories are funny, engaging, thought-provoking and inspiring, and he helps us see that we are all connected through our energy and creative potential. He helps me see my relationship to my God-given creativity differently. The source of everything is always there for us to tap into at any moment. I have used this book to change my work, my relationships and my life."

~ **Tina Quinn,** author of *Invisible Things*

***

"*CREATOR* is magic in print! I was completely captivated (and thoroughly entertained) by how Steve Chandler effortlessly floats between spiritually profound and real-world practicality and helps us navigate it all along the way. *CREATOR* breaks down the walls of our 'conditioning' (even his take on THAT concept created a big shift for me) and introduces us to a life made more prosperous, more fun, more fulfilling and more joyful through the always-available-on-demand power of our creativity!"

~ **Jason Goldberg,** author of *Prison Break*

CREATOR

CREATOR
STEVE CHANDLER

MAURICE BASSETT

CREATOR

Maurice Bassett
P.O. Box 839
Anna Maria, FL 34216

Contact the publisher:
MauriceBassett@gmail.com
www.MauriceBassett.com

Contact the author:
www.SteveChandler.com

Editing: Kathy Eimers Chandler
Assistant editor and interior layout: Chris Nelson
Cover design: Carrie Brito
Cover art: *Reflections* by Mandy Goss

ISBN: 978-1-60025-131-3

Library of Congress Control Number: 2018914646

First Edition

To Kathy

She was in awe of all his work.
"How do you do it?" she asked.
He smiled and said, "By loving you."

~ **Kamand Kojouri**

Appreciation

I want to express my gratitude:

To Fred Knipe for ongoing creative consultation and our indispensable friendship. To Mandy Goss for the wonderful work of art on the cover. To Maurice Bassett for publishing and Kathy Eimers Chandler and Chris Nelson for editing.

To Carrie Brito for artistic design. To Michael Neill for co-facilitating the creative writing workshops with me. To Steve Hardison for the ultimate in transformational coaching.

To Dicken Bettinger, Mark Howard and Garret Kramer for mentoring and guidance. And to the inspirational members of the M6: Karen Davis, Kamin Samuel, Carolyn Freyer-Jones, Devon Bandison, Tina Quinn and Mo Baldwin.

Table of Contents

CREATOR

Real art comes from the ultimate, from a vision; from the spirit, as Beethoven would say; from God, as Bach would say.

~ Francis Lucille

INTRODUCTION

Something better than heaven?

There is something better than heaven. It is the eternal, meaningless, infinitely creative mind. It can't stop for time or space or even joy. It is so brilliant that it will shake what's left of you to the depths of all-consuming wonder.

~ Byron Katie

You read that quote and wonder. What is she saying? Does she mean *my* mind? Or does she mean some kind of universal mind? The bottomless well of creativity that Napoleon Hill called "infinite intelligence"? Or is it all the same?

Wouldn't that be exciting, though, to discover something better than heaven and to have that discovery shake me to the depths?

So I wondered how she could say that with such relaxed certainty. Would she be trying to sell us some new-age product or course? That would be a cynic's view, which is to say it would be *my* view when first I encountered this claim of hers that there was something better than heaven.

A cynic will hear something like this and start to get excited, but then will stop himself. His conditioning has kicked in. What about these bills and these kids to care for? What about all the books and essays I have read by the highly intelligent philosophers of existential despair? Didn't they convince me that the "human condition" was essentially negative?

Yes they did, and it matched up nicely with how I perceived my own condition.

But then things changed, and I began to see that my "condition" was actually only my conditioning.

But what's the difference? Seems like there's no difference.

Here it is: When people like me talk about their "conditioning" they speak of it as if it stopped somewhere. Usually in childhood. That's where conditioning solidifies into the human condition. Or so we're told.

There was conditioning that was caused by what I was taught and how I was raised, and then the conditioning came to completion. After that, for the rest of my life I would be stuck with how I was conditioned. I would refer to it as "my conditioning." It would never change. How could it? It was over and complete.

Inside that story, I had been conditioned just as a piece of meat gets marinated. I'd be sitting in a Polynesian restaurant eating marinated chunks of steak telling you about my childhood and my conditioning as if they were one and the same.

What could be wrong with that story? What is it I didn't know, that if I knew it, might change the game of life forever?

This is what it was:

Conditioning never stops.

Conditioning is ongoing. I'm not marinated meat. I am literally always like a culinary work in progress. Each day is full of possibility. The menu is always new.

Conditioning is continuous. What I did and saw and learned this morning is as vital a part of my ongoing conditioning as the conditioning that occurred in childhood. In fact, today's conditioning is even more vital than my childhood conditioning, especially if it takes me in new directions. Especially when it counters and replaces earlier conditioning.

When I looked back on my life there was more than enough evidence of this. I had been conditioned to believe that drinking alcohol made life better. Then I was conditioned to believe, after I descended into alcoholism, that the only way I could get relief from the pain of living was through drinking and drugs.

But then I joined a program and got a sponsor and created the mental space and spiritual openness for an entirely new conditioning to drop in. This resulted in a total transformation of my relationship to life and people.

And this wasn't childhood. This was my access to ongoing conditioning. Something I didn't know I had. I didn't realize that when it came to conditioning I was now able to assume my rightful role as *creator*. I was now in charge of it. And that wasn't the case in childhood.

So this morning I read the words of Byron Katie and reflect on them. I relax enough to see the truth in them. And I think of my first response to her teaching years ago and understand why it was so pessimistic and dismissive.

People don't change was my core belief. I was stuck with my weaknesses and faults. My job was to try to hide them if I was to have a life. I had to hide—or distract you from—my traits and characteristics. My identity worked against me. And because this was true for me, my first response to Katie was that her words were unreal. (It was a conditioned response.)

But then through a spiritual program of recovery I saw that I could respond differently. I decided to explore. Byron Katie had devised a little meditative system for the deletion of negative conditioning. She explains it in her first book, *Loving What Is*. She called her system "The Work."

Before I bought her book, I noticed on the cover that

Eckhart Tolle had said, "Byron Katie's Work acts like a razor-sharp sword that cuts through . . . illusion and enables you to know for yourself the timeless essence of your being. Joy, peace, and love emanate from it as your natural state. In *Loving What Is*, you have the key. Now use it."

That quote hit me hard because I'd already become a fan of Tolle's book *The Power of Now*. Why would he make that kind of statement? It seemed to go beyond praise for a book. It was as if he was describing a magical garden tool. He wasn't saying how much he enjoyed the book. He was telling me to *use it*.

What would I be digging up?

Well, it turned out to be just about everything. All my old conditioning. All the defeated and pessimistic neural pathways. All the old thoughts mistakenly assumed to be the truth about life.

And why did it work for me? Because I did it. I followed the simple directions. The Work worked just the same way it worked for Katie, as she writes and talks about. She was just sharing what worked for her. She was not putting out some new thing to try to believe in. It will work for you too. And it's not the only path.

Byron Katie had a flash of revelation one morning and saw what so many "enlightened" people have seen (all the great religious figures in the past, on up to Ramana Maharshi, Sydney Banks, Douglas Harding, Werner Erhard, Mooji, Eckhart Tolle, Rupert Spira, Francis Lucille and on and on). She saw life as pure love and light.

But then her thoughts started coming back in. All the old conditioning. So she *created* her system she called The Work. It worked for her. It revealed thought to be what it was, and so thought was no longer the great truth about life. And she promised everyone she worked with and taught her system to that if they were courageous enough to stay with it to the very end, they too would see clearly that "There is something better than heaven. It is the eternal, meaningless, infinitely creative mind."

Hers is but one path back to the realization and occupation of the infinitely creative mind. There are many others, both spiritual and psychological. I'll put some of the most effective books and teachers in the *Recommended Reading* section at the end. These are based on my own experience and the experience of people I work with.

My clients want to believe in what Katie sees and what Syd Banks and Ramana Maharshi and other spiritual philosophers saw. But their conditioning keeps chattering the old pessimistic mantras. And I can relate to them completely. I wanted to believe, too. I would listen to Alan Watts say, "No valid plans for the *future* can be made by those who have no *capacity* for living now," and I would think, "Okay there go my plans for the future. And I thought the future was going to save me."

I was wanting to believe I could experience joy and creativity in living now, but I wasn't seeing that it was not a matter of belief. It was a matter of experience.

When I was a little boy I wanted to believe the deep end of the pool water would hold me up, but my conditioned thought chatter said, "Don't go there, you're heavier than water."

My mistake was staying stuck inside wanting to believe deep water would hold me up. I didn't realize that belief had nothing to do with it. In fact, belief and disbelief were the things that were holding me back. Stalling things out. Familiarity with the water was all I needed in order to reveal the truth of it.

Both believers and non-believers (in my head) can step aside as I jump in. They are only in the way.

To live in the world of creation—to get into it and stay in it—to frequent it and haunt it—to think intently and fruitfully—to woo combinations and inspirations into being by a depth and continuity of attention and meditation—this is the only thing.

~ Henry James

And a hero comes along

Throughout my boyhood I loved comic book superheroes, as so many children do. Mighty Mouse, Superman, and Captain Marvel filled my dreams. I had the comic books and watched the TV episodes and always felt a surge of excitement picturing myself with their powers.

When I began growing into adulthood the superheroes lost their pull. Adulthood was getting harder and harder for me to navigate, and those old heroes were just fantasies, right? I needed to get into reality. (One thesaurus I looked at recently had a lot of synonyms for the word *creativity* but only one antonym. The antonym they listed was "*reality*.")

I needed to deal with my lack of power that seemed to accompany growing up.

That was the thinking that was circulating inside me back then. And when my not-so-super life of bad choices got too heavy to hold up, I finally hit bottom. I found myself in recovery meetings for alcoholics where we admitted we were powerless over alcohol and that our lives had become unmanageable. I had become Powerless Man. A long way from Superman.

Or so I thought at the time.

But then, little by little, with recovery adding more light

each day, I began to wake up. I was free of addiction for the first time and the world began to open up in front of me. More and more often I found myself in good spirits. I was attending meetings about spiritual recovery in which we explored and practiced "conscious contact with a higher power." It was all new to me. But it was real, practical experience. Not just something one hopes for.

It was truly recovery . . . not just from alcohol but from what my meetings called "self-will run riot." It felt like the ego was fading out while the light of recovery unfolded like a blanket of stars.

It wasn't until much later that I saw that my (and our) higher power (the God of our understanding) was creativity itself.

Before it made its real appearance, I had always liked the *word* "creativity," and I had bought into the prevailing belief that it was a rare and precious thing. I also noticed that my ego really liked it when people said I, as an individual personality, was creative. Really? You mean that? I took it very personally. I remember being extremely proud of myself when I was named "Creative Director" of an advertising agency. How special it felt to be seen as creative! And not just creative, but so creative that they want you to be the *Director* of creativity! I was captivated by how *unique* I was becoming and—really— how exceptional I must be! I guess I'll just have to learn to accept that I'm *one of the rare few* who have access to this form of magic we all call creativity!

But my thoughts weren't really matching up with reality. Deep down I knew it. My belief (and the belief of those around me) that creativity was an uncommon personal gift began to lose its credibility. I could soon see that it was a story, like so many of my other stories, designed to keep the ego feeling unique. But it had nothing to do with real creativity. Or real and true reality—no matter what my thesaurus and my culture said.

The more spiritual work and study I did the more I saw that creativity and the life force were one and the same. And it was a force running through everybody, not just the chosen creative few. In our recovery meetings we all had a higher power, higher than the ego, and higher than human thought.

Here we were, a group of alcoholics and drug addicts sitting together trying to learn to live a normal, clean and sober life . . . and one sign on the meeting hall wall said, "Your best thinking got you here."

We weren't sages; we were drunks. But we were experiencing the same kind of higher power that the sages wrote about. A power without upper limits. You could call it a superpower—just what I longed for as a kid. Maybe my yearning and longing and reaching out for Superman as a boy was not a total delusion.

If I wrote an adventure comic book today I would see if I could introduce a new superhero—which would be no small thing given how many superheroes there already are: Wonder Woman, Iron Man, Supergirl, Daredevil, Batman, and you know we could go on.

My comic book's superhero would be you.

I know that's not a really exciting or marketable name for a superhero. "You!"

No, so let's call you something else. How about this. Do you know how movies always acknowledge the "creator" of various superhero characters? For example, Wonder Woman's creator was William Marston. Imagine how powerful he must have been. It's one thing to be Wonder Woman, but it's quite another to be able to *create* Wonder Woman.

If these characters like Wonder Woman and Superman and Mighty Mouse are so powerful, just imagine how much more powerful their creators must be. That's the ultimate superpower right there: the ability to create.

I'd call that hero "Creator."

And the adventures I'd present would show you that it's all based on a true story: the story of you.

I'm always thinking about creating. My future starts when I wake up every morning . . . Every day I find something creative to do with my life.

~ Miles Davis

Are you really not creative?

People who tell me they are "not creative" cause me to wonder. Could that ever be true?

Perhaps they have not found a consistent expression of creativity. But there is no shortage on the inside. Not in my experience.

It would be like going to a doctor because of shortness of breath and having the doctor say, "I'm sorry to have to tell you that you have no lungs."

If you are alive enough to hear the doctor, you are breathing, and you do have lungs. In the same way, if you are alive enough to be reading this and wondering, you are creative.

In fact, it goes even deeper than that. You're not just a person who has this characteristic called "creative" among your many other qualities, such as "affectionate" or "sensitive." Because it's *not* just a quality that you may or may not have.

What you think of as "you" is creativity itself.

Creativity! Prior to, and way beyond thought. And driving and dwarfing all those things we see as qualities.

Is it hard to accept? Hard to let in? The fact that creativity is who you are and all you are?

If you can see that people are noticing you are "affectionate" and "sensitive," well, maybe you can know it's because the spirit that is you is *creating* those things.

So don't let anyone tell you that you can't create. Especially don't let your inner voices tell you that.

When they say that, they are speaking to creativity itself! They are speaking into the very whirlwind their words claim is absent. They point out a lack of water in you while being drenched by your firehose. They are crying wolf at you! They are shouting "FIRE!" into your crowded theater. They are pissing into the wind. They are trying to nail Jell-O to the wall. They are trying to shovel mercury with a pitchfork.

They are saying you are not creative!

Forgive them! They know not what they do. They don't get who you are.

Every breath you breathe is an act of creation. Every thought you think. And you can take it from there. Expand it and express it. Paint it all on the ceiling of your cathedral and into the calendar of your life.

Or you can turn your back on it forever and call that adulthood.

But even if you do that, I know who you are, so I'll not call you by the name your parents chose for you and filed with the government. The name *I'll* use for you is creator. I hope you're uncomfortable with that. At least for a while.

Can you see the possibility here? Can you see that in relationship to all your wins, losses, situations, trials, celebrations and sorrows you are creator? That's who you are. That's what you are.

You might think this is veering toward, "You created this mess, you yourself, so don't come running to me to get you out of it."

Of course there's always some truth in that, but I'm more interested in the bigger, wilder picture—the really exciting opportunity you have to discard your government name and take on your true, reality-based identity.

Creator.

When the world turned its back on me
I was up against the wall
I had no foundation
No friends and no family to catch my fall
Running on empty, with nothing left in me
    but doubt
I picked up a pen
and wrote my way out

~ Nas, Dave East, Lin-Manual Miranda
& Aloe Blacc
"I Wrote My Way Out"

Let me try to be honest

Now I'm going to stop talking to you.

Because it just hit me: I'm actually talking to myself here. Why do I always seem to do that? I try to teach other people things I myself need to learn but haven't even started to learn.

I was saying things to you like, "You're more than that" and "The really exciting opportunity you have"—as if I know something you don't know and I'm teaching it to you.

But I'm talking to myself. I'm putting down the words that I need to see. For myself. For personal reasons. Maybe it helps you, too, and if so I'm pleased with that, but this is really my own learning going on here.

Although I'm seeing that I'm really talking to myself, I can still imagine what you're thinking. It's like I can hear your thoughts knocking around in here. And I know you are questioning all of this.

Let me ask you something. I know you've often thought you were not all that creative. And it might have hurt you when you believed that. And it's hard, isn't it, to honor that hurt? And to continue to nurse it throughout your life?

But what if that thought itself were later revealed to be totally and transparently untrue? What if every negative thought you ever had was untrue? What if your own creativity was limitless?

Okay but aren't some people more creative than others?

No. By which I mean: yes, in a sense—but not really.

Some people have learned to express their innate creativity in more dramatic and memorable ways than others, but don't let that throw you off. That can really throw people off. It can give them the wrong idea. Seeing something profoundly beautiful and moving created by another creator can lead to the false belief that you are not also a creator.

If I see someone in the Olympics lift a tremendous amount of weight I don't automatically believe I can't lift. I don't stare down at my glass of water and not drink it, not lift it up to my mouth, just because I saw that guy lift so much weight. Do I? When I'm really thirsty?

My wife: "Why aren't you drinking your water? I thought you were really thirsty?"

Me: "Will you pour it in my mouth?"

"What, why? Why can't you just drink it?"

"I can't lift."

"You can't lift what?"

"I can't lift the glass."

"Why not?"

"I'm not a lifter. Not at all. Not even close to being a lifter. Why am I not a lifter? Because I saw that Olympic lifter. *He* was a lifter. That's what *real* lifting looks like, and so that's what lifting *is*."

Absurd? Yes, but it's everywhere: I don't paint because of Van Gogh. I don't dance because of Michael Jackson. I don't sing because of Elvis.

Right? I won't dance—don't ask me!

This thought process is exactly where my potential for creative expression dies: right into my comparisons.

Actually that's not quite right. My creativity never dies. It never goes anywhere. It's always fully present. My *awareness* of it is what disappears, so my *access* simultaneously disappears.

They disappear into self-judgment. They disappear into thought.

What we often forget is that thought is to be used to correct life. It's *not* a way of life! If you make thought the center of your life, you're not going to live it.

~ **Ray Bradbury**

But what if this were life itself?

I set my glass of water aside and open the book I'm reading (for the third time) by Brenda Ueland, called *If You Want to Write*. In it she says (and I see I have highlighted it in yellow) William Blake has inspired her on this subject of expressing creativity. Blake said, "Imagination is the Divine Body in every person."

Brenda Ueland then says, "Blake thought that this creative power should be kept alive in all people for all of their lives. And so do I. Why? Because it is life itself. It is the spirit. In fact it is the only important thing about us. The rest of us is legs and stomach, materialistic cravings and fears."

Because of how her book wakes me up, I'm feeling real gratitude for this brilliant woman. I see that this book of hers was written in 1938! Yet after I read some of her book, this day today feels like a new morning: and I see that life is for creation. I don't have to turn on the news and become a *reactor* in life. I don't have to read what some politician or actor said and go nuclear. Not when I'm basking in the yellow-highlighted truth of this book.

You don't need a paintbrush to be creative. Your own unique perspective is your brush.

You don't need an instrument to be creative. Your body-mind is your instrument.

You don't need a canvas to be creative. Your friends and family and relationships are your canvas.

You don't need a masterpiece or grand theory to be creative. Your life is your masterpiece.

~ Corey W. deVos

A quick peek behind the curtain

People who have near-death experiences come back to tell us that this whole universe is a beautiful field made up entirely of love. And it's one love . . . all just one love.

Bob Marley sang us the same message with the words, "One love, one heart, let's get together and feel alright." No wonder his songs had names like "Natural Mystic" and "Wake Up and Live."

Many others have had direct, experiential encounters with this energy field, even without the body's dying first. Some call it "God" or "The Great Spirit," and some said it was enlightenment or Nirvana. It has had many names—reflecting the powerlessness of human vocabularies to nail it down.

Some received their experience by way of devotional religious practices and others through years of deep meditation. But sometimes people got it by receiving some kind of whack upside the soul.

However people find it out, the experience is no longer just found in the writings of ancient sages and saints. It seems to be happening more often to "ordinary" people we can relate to, like Sydney Banks, Eckhart Tolle, Dicken Bettinger, Jean Klein, Ramana Maharshi, Byron Katie, Rupert Spira, Werner Erhard. . . The list of the "enlightened" few is rapidly becoming the "enlightened" many.

The near-death reports back from the other side are remarkably similar. People saw the light and then saw that we *are* the light. Their experiences seem to suggest that we are created by the Creator in the image of the Creator, and therefore we were born to create.

What if you and I, just average people having an average day, truly saw, moment to moment, that that was true?

What would be left to sing but "Hallelujah!"? (We could sing that with Handel or Leonard Cohen or everyone in between.)

It seems to be easier for people returning from physical death to wake up to the creative joy of life, but what about the rest of us? Do we just turn green with enlightenment envy? It's not that easy being green, feeling like we're in exile from that far off spiritual energy field. I can sure feel like that—I'm green with spiritual envy and in the dark out here, a million miles from the joyful in-crowd.

But to realize my creative power I have to let the feeling that I'm in the dark just pass through. I have to consider the possibility that I'm not all that separate and isolated from spiritual teachers, saints and gurus. Maybe that separation is just a story I've heard and bought into and, through repetition, converted into an entire felt sense of how the world is.

Me? The creative source itself?

Come on, let's get real.

The story of my separate, dull, egoic self disconnected from divine creativity gets continually supported by the collective belief system of the culture. It's approved continuously by acclamation and then fed back to us through the virtual reality of the media, the schools and the entertainment channels.

The truth is—rather, I should say, my experience tells me—

that we non-saints see the light too. We all do. Sometimes it's just now and then, here and there, but divine light shines through and we see it.

But then most of us don't know what to make of it! We think it's just a momentary flash of happiness. Out of nowhere, a lucky, accidental moment worth treasuring. These are simply moments to remember! And just as we believe our own story of separation, we also think those flashing moments of joy and light are also separate. Contained. Isolated. Independent. Safely sealed off like a biohazard would be.

We don't even consider that that the flashing light we see might be trying to tell us something. In those moments when we feel something true or beautiful, the light of creativity might well be trying to peek through our web of beliefs to show us the source of everything . . . and to let us know that it's always there for us. And if that's so, then maybe creativity itself may be the very energy that words like "eternal" and "infinite" were made up to describe.

The light of creativity can appear in ordinary moments. It can happen when you're writing a note or listening to music or singing a song or laughing at your bad, little dog. For that brief, shining moment it can even feel like the old song that says, "When you're laughing, the sun comes shining through."

If enough of those moments were seen truly and clearly it would become obvious to you that the entire universe was set up to correct you from—and talk you out of—thinking and believing this single thought: "I am not creative."

The sun came shining through once again for me on this subject this morning. My flash of light came when reading today's "Gmorning" tweet from Lin-Manuel Miranda, creator of the revolutionary hip hop musical *Hamilton*:

Gmorning.
Breathe deep.

That hitch in your breath is a record scratch.
That throbbing in your temple is the bass, and you control
    the volume knob.
The scars in your mind and your heart are grooves that
    run deep.
YOUR music. YOUR heart. YOUR life. You got the
    aux cord.
Bump it.

His tweets inspire and encourage multitudes of people. Because they're not about him. (And they're not about politicians.) They're about the creative power of you. And me. And all people. Why else would they be so popular?

With the whole world trying to isolate him, separate him, single him out as a creative genius, he replies with the opposite message. He says *you*. You've got it too. So don't sleep on that. You've got the cord.

Now bump it.

And when the night is cloudy,
there is still a light that shines on me.

~ Lennon and McCartney
"Let It Be"

You say you want a revelation

One of my flashes of light occurred while sitting in a circle of people in group therapy around thirty years ago. And this wasn't a little flash.

This was the sun.

I had joined the talk therapy group to receive support for something upsetting I was going through in my family. I thought the group could help me not feel so all alone with my trouble. And it did. It was a wonderful experience of togetherness, as in Bob Marley's "Let's get together and feel alright."

The trouble in my life revolved around my late wife, the mother of my children. She suffered from a dissociative disorder then called "multiple personality." None of us knew she had this condition until an incident occurred at a treatment center where she was attending a workshop on "codependency." The facilitators told me she broke down completely and demonstrated psychotic trauma and dangerous behavior, and if I waited a few days I might be able to visit her in the intensive care ward of the mental institution they had put her in.

This was a rather big "Say what?" for me and the four children. It was a shock to our lives and a deeply painful and terrifying experience for *her*. She spent the next year and a half in and out of the institution and in and out of therapy. The children and I were perpetually scared and worried. All the various personalities who were "not our mom" tried to interact with us and deal with the painful strangeness of it all. Sometimes she would disappear for days and none of us, including her, knew where she had been.

I wasn't sleeping. My sense of safety and well-being was gone. I still had my sobriety, thank God (I mean that), and those brave little children under my care, but I was a neurotic mess, and so I joined the therapy group.

As the months went by, I learned more and more from my wife's psychiatric doctors that she had been badly abused as a little girl and taken into a Satanic cult where the abuse intensified. They explained to me that the brain has the capacity to create subpersonalities when the primary personality suffers from memories that are unbearable. Those subpersonalities, or "alters," now live in separate realities with separate memory systems. So they will have no recollection of the abuse.

The problem comes in (and becomes an official "disorder") when the brain starts creating more and more personalities once it knows it can. Soon it's creating new "people" to deal with every little discomfort the other "people" can't handle.

I don't mean to make light of any of this or not acknowledge the pain that came with the confusion and chaos. Although sometimes, to save my sanity, I'd try to show humor . . . I said to a friend once that I kept the TV channel changer at my side, and if a difficult personality appeared I'd reach for it, point it her way, and start clicking.

(I get that that's not funny. You don't have to reach out to me on social media about it.)

But if the whole situation wasn't funny, it was certainly

amazing. That began to really sink in for me. Especially after the year and a half of chaos and upset passed and she began to get better and better. (To hold inside a single created self.) I began to be able to reflect on the whole experience and what it might have revealed.

Because somehow, through her therapy and her own strong will to live and "heal," the disorderly aspect of the disorder faded away, and she was able to see the children on a part-time basis and they were able to get the mom back that they loved.

And one day, as I sat in my group therapy circle feeling love and gratitude for all these compassionate people who had helped me through these troubled times, I had a vision. It just descended out of nowhere as a silent voice that came inside my own voice as I looked out at the people in the circle who were looking back at me. My voice then said, "We are the multiple personalities of God."

Some of the people laughed and some looked startled, and I was trying to understand what I had just said to them. They wanted me to say more, and all I could say was that it was something I could just feel and see in that moment of love and gratitude for them, that it was *one spirit* simultaneously appearing as each of us, playing all the parts.

Most of them felt sorry for me. They didn't see what I was saying, and one older guy said, "You've had a rough go of it with this whole multiple personality thing so I can see why you have it on the brain right now. Get some rest. You'll be fine."

But I never forgot that moment.

And I never forgot the clarity of that vision. I've told almost no one about that day until now. And I never thought I'd be telling you or anyone else about it until the thing that happened two days ago happened.

Promise me tonight....
That when you take to the streets,
You're on your way to the skies.
When night is bringing the end,
You're running into the light.

~ **Lacy Wilder**
"Into the Light"

It could happen to you

"Hide your heart from sight.
Lock your dreams at night.
It could happen to you."

(I hear Jo Stafford singing those words as I type.)

What happened to me two days ago was this: I was casually looking through *Scientific American* magazine to see if they had an article by a writer I like. When I found that they did, I looked at the article's headline and saw this:

"Could Multiple Personality Disorder Explain Life,
the Universe and Everything?"

I had to turn away from that headline and then look twice. Really?

Yes indeed. It did say that.

And it was an article by one of my favorite contemporary authors, Bernardo Kastrup. He was both a scientist and a philosopher, and his books about culture, neuroscience and consciousness had become my latest reading obsessions.

As I looked at that headline again, and the question it asked, I immediately thought back to the flash of vision I'd had decades ago in my therapy group. And that unexpected thing I saw and said: that we are the multiple personalities of God.

Kastrup and the article's co-authors, Adam Crabtree and Edward F. Kelly, cited extensive studies of patients with this disorder (now called Dissociative Identity Disorder, or DID) in which functional brain scans are used to show that subpersonalities have their own separate areas in the brain—and are therefore not just "acting as if" they were different people.

Kastrup and his co-authors write:

Although we may be at a loss to explain precisely how this creative process occurs (because it unfolds almost totally beyond the reach of self-reflective introspection) the clinical evidence nevertheless forces us to acknowledge something is happening that has important implications for our views about what is and is not possible in nature.

As disorienting and shocking an experience as it was in real life for me to be talking to different people occupying the same body, it might even be more amazing to look back dispassionately and realize the power of what the researchers call "this creative process."

The *Scientific American* writers conclude:

We know empirically from DID that consciousness can give rise to many operationally distinct centers of concurrent experience, each with its own personality and sense of identity. Therefore, if something analogous to DID happens at a universal level, the one universal consciousness could, as a result, give rise to many alters with private inner lives like yours and ours. *As such, we may all be alters—dissociated personalities—of universal consciousness.*

Knock me over with a feather. *Scientific American* has just said, in their own way, that we're all the multiple personalities of God. They may call it "universal consciousness creating subpersonalities of itself," but I don't want to split hairs.

Whatever words we choose, it's becoming as clear to science as it has been for millennia to spiritual philosophers that divine, universal creativity is the source and substance of everything, including and especially who we think we are.

It gives me greater understanding of why my friend and life coach Steve Hardison used to ask me two questions, over and over in the course of our work together. When I described a problematic situation in my life, he would listen carefully and then say, "Okay, given that that's the situation, what would you like to create?"

Notice that it was not "How do you want to solve it?" As if the problem itself had all the power. As if the problem were a bomb we had to carefully disarm. He never saw the problem as having the power in the situation. He always saw creativity as having all the power. And together we didn't really have to "solve" anything. We didn't need to. What we created made the problems fade from all relevance.

And the second question he'd always ask me would appear whenever it didn't look like I could do some scary thing I needed to do. Instead of telling me what I needed to do, he would always ask me, "Who do you need to be?" Because he always knew, and I learned through practice, that I could create that being. I could create who I needed to be.

(It's all we ever do anyway.)

When you understand who and what you are, your radiance projects into the universal radiance, and everything around you becomes creative and full of opportunity.

~ **Yogi Bhajan**

Okay but how do I create?

It took me many years to learn that the answer to "How do I create?" was . . . to create. To jump into the work. Jump into the waters. Then let innovation flow in from beyond thought.

Keep moving inside the work. Don't be afraid to open up to beyond what's known. The best ideas eventually come from there. Not directly from "trying to figure this out."

The only thing that *trying to figure it out* does is serve as a functional folly. Like the old saying, "A fool who persists in his folly will become wise." If that's true, then the folly of the left brain trying hard to figure this out is actually useful!

Because you give up. Eventually. And that's a form of surrender. To the bigger picture. To universal consciousness. To the source of creativity.

So as Creator you are willing to become the fool who persists.

When my left brain is trying to figure out the creative process it is only useful for how it will bring me into a fully played-out experience of futility. Running on empty. I think of Bob Dylan's song, "Too Much of Nothing." My ego's personalized and repetitive thinking becomes too much of nothing, and it then leads me into a strange place that song talks about: "the waters of oblivion."

The waters of oblivion! Sounds so hopeless.

But for a creator the waters of oblivion can also represent the divine unknowing. A great place to be. The most fertile place there is.

Most adults don't believe that. Which is why they don't openly and expressively create what they could. They fear the unknown and revere the known. Because for them the unknown represents ignorance and weakness. So they only work with what they know. The last thing they want to be seen as is *someone who doesn't know what they're doing!*

They forget that when they were a child they didn't know what they were doing and it was the best time ever.

What did Jesus mean when he said, "Truly I tell you, whoever does not receive the kingdom of God like a little child will never enter it"?

An artful and prolific creator like Picasso has a child-like playfulness going on in his work. The first thing he said he did before he entered his studio was turn back his internal clock to when he was a child. It gave him access to the unknown. From there he could see heaven in a blazingly colorful wildflower. He was no longer clinging to just a fragment of localized, personalized consciousness. He could paint from universal consciousness.

To Picasso, *not knowing* was not only safe, but it was where everything creative was coming from.

Do not fear mistakes.
There are none.

~ **Miles Davis**

A little boy in a highchair

My grandson at eighteen months was sitting in his highchair eating macaroni and cheese. He playfully put two little tubes of macaroni on his forehead above his eyebrows and smiled at us—a wicked little smile—he'd made new macaroni eyebrows!

The grownups laughed. They loved it. It was so delightful.

Grownups standing around the highchair with careful, neat haircuts. Grownups with make-up on for perfect faces and eyebrows sculpted to frozen perfection. Cautious, frozen adults, like ice sculptures, fingers on the pause-button of life. Tightly wrapped up in their carefully-fitted zones of safety. Ready to react. Always ready to react. In fact, in their minds, born to react.

So different than the little boy in the highchair. Open to anything. Up for any game. Born to create.

All the grownups were once there in that same highchair. Alive with creativity. But now, today, when they laughed with delight at the playful little boy they didn't call what he did "creativity." And they certainly didn't call it "natural, innate, inborn creativity." They called it macaroni.

You've got to keep the child alive;
you can't create without it.

~ Joni Mitchell

Flowing through your every move

If you're like most adults I know (including me much of the time), you probably have no idea about the fountain of creativity behind everything you do and think. Behind every breath, and every heartbeat, flowing through your every move and non-move.

You might think (just like I usually do) that creativity is a special quality or ability that some people have and some don't. Maybe you'll admit that you have a little of it, but it only comes through when you do water colors or noodle at the piano, create a new recipe or write a little poem for your friend's birthday.

But you don't see the whole fountain. You experience a water drop or two thrown off. But that's all.

My wish for you (and me) is that from now on we use those drops of water to remind us of the whole and infinite fountain.

May your heart always be joyful.
May your song always be sung.

~ Bob Dylan
"Forever Young"

Which energy do you want?

After I had stumbled upon the discovery that we all have massive amounts of creativity poised in the space prior to thought, ready to serve us and express great beauty, I wanted to try to work that awareness into what I was teaching my business clients.

And of course people told me, "Good luck with that."

But why not try?

So I'd go into a company that hired me to help increase performance and productivity and teach a course I'd often called "Owner versus Victim" but was now calling "Creator versus Reactor." Because I knew my clients liked binary distinctions and new ways to label themselves and others, I decided to meet them where they were and indulge their preferences.

I stared at them from the front of the room and said, "You can always make a choice, no matter what challenge arises. You can be a creator . . . or you can be a reactor!"

We looked at various problems and situations they were facing in their work, and we explored the differences between responding creatively to the situation versus just reacting emotionally. They began to see that when they stayed upbeat in the awareness of creativity, they could be a creator who designs a solution. Conversely, if they took on a victim mindset and began to take impersonal situations personally they would become unproductive, stressed out and fatigued.

They began seeing new ways of creating what they wanted instead of falling into their old habits of reacting to what they didn't want. One older guy went to my whiteboard during a break and under where I had written "a creator or a reactor" he wrote, "a designer or a whiner?"

That itself was creative. I was glad they were getting it.

The beneficial application of creativity in real company situations wasn't hard to see. If a key employee quits, you can spend hours worrying and complaining about "what a bind" that leaves you in. You can vent to anyone who will listen, at work and at home, about how hard it is to replace good people and how blindsided you were by the employee's departure.

That's you being a reactor. You can say to anyone who knows about the situation and who passes you in the hall, "This is the last thing I needed!" Other reactors will support you in staying inside that energy and treating it like the truth.

But there's different energy available. Much more wild and powerful. And it comes to you the minute you become a creator.

And you can do this with *any* "problem" that arises in your life. You can ask yourself, "Given the facts of this situation, what would I like to create?"

You might get on the phone and create the kinds of conversations and communications that lead you to a perfect replacement for the departed employee.

You might later create a whole new hiring and recruiting system that gives you a "waiting list" of good people.

The point is this: creativity is always there for you. And it turns life around faster than anything else.

Why do people have to pay a coach in order to "learn" this late in life? If it's an energy field always there for everyone, why does it have to be pointed out and "taught"? I mean, I'm a bright enough person. Why did I not discover the true potential of this awareness until so late in my life?

Our society and our culture don't seem to recognize it yet. So in schools and at home we only learn how to figure things out and how to best react to all the things we could be confronted by. We also learn that creativity is for the rare, chosen few. Creative talent is weirdly unique and almost always gets attached to the concept of genius.

Van Gogh? Creative genius. You and me? Don't make me laugh.

So our intellect goes along with the crowd. When things get challenging we complain and react. We have learned to do that from the people around us all our lives. Therefore it's not surprising that we don't access creativity in the face of a new situation. Any new twist or turn in the flow of life and we respond like reactors: "Well, *this* sucks."

Once that thought hits the brain (and is believed) it can cast off more discouraging thoughts, until your thought process looks like the blood-spatter pattern at a homicide scene. The more I think this way, the worse it gets. My mood and enthusiasm for life start to roll down and form a drip pattern that the investigators must label: *reactor*.

I said to my seminar attendees, "You can continue to be a part of that victim energy for the rest of your life if you want to. Or you can create. The choice is always yours."

It wasn't such a hard sell once we'd run through a lot of their questions and challenges. We learned to take the raw material of a complaint and from that create a request. We learned to take the request and out of that create an agreement. It turned out that people *loved* seeing all the applications of the creator/reactor choice. It pointed them back to larger sources of intelligence than their egoic minds and showed them they could always stay open to a continuous flow of fresh ideas.

Back then all of that was sufficiently exciting. To them and to me. And because it was so effective I was able to get it into a lot of corporations and other organizations who would otherwise have labeled that training and coaching as "soft" or "spiritual" or "new-age nonsense."

At that time I don't think they (or I!) saw how big the picture really was. We were happy enough choosing between the labels of creator and reactor without even imagining the scope and depth of the infinite divine potential that was there. I didn't see, back then, that creators were people who were courageously allowing their *true nature* to shine through and create. And that reactors were merely people who obsessed over the obstacles (known as beliefs) to their awareness of who they really were.

You can fume at the world if you like. You can also use your words, art and gifts to let us in. Build us a bridge to where you are.

~ **Lin-Manuel Miranda**

Letting your love light shine

My friend Christopher was a devoted teacher of spiritual psychology and told me more than once that he believed that deep down he was "divine, loving, creative energy." He said he believed everyone was.

But I noticed that most of the time he *lived* as if he was anything but that.

He lived as if he was only a contracted, egoic personality filled with shame and flaws and self-doubt. When something wasn't going the way he wanted it to, he personalized it. He went immediately into, "What's wrong with me?"

One time he realized that he had not talked to his sister in many months. So he immediately tried to figure out what was wrong. What's wrong with a person who didn't stay connected to his own sister? *What's that about? I have to figure that out!*

The more he worried about the human qualities he might lack, the worse he felt and the less he felt like calling his sister. After all, if there was something wrong with him, something broken in him, and it was *causing* this "cold-hearted" behavior, wouldn't that have to be fixed and solved before he reached out to his sister? If he called his sister now it would be a call filled with apology and remorse, and then (because of whatever personal flaw this was) he would probably go many more months without calling her again, and that would just make matters worse.

The people who knew Christopher and listened to his self-criticism sometimes felt like saying, "Just call your f*@king sister!"

But that wouldn't have been a final solution for Christopher. Because it would have been skipping over the most important missing piece in all of this: awareness.

Christopher wasn't aware. He had no realization. He didn't even have an understanding. Christopher might have "believed" (when you asked him in a spiritual setting) that he was "loving, creative energy," but he wasn't actually *aware* that he was.

When you're aware of something, you know it on a level beyond thought and belief. It's a feeling that permeates everything. When you are aware that the rain is falling, you don't have to try to believe that the rain is falling.

Christopher was trying to believe.

When someone is *aware* of what they really are—the pure radiant light of creative energy—they just live as an expression of that awareness. Positive action happens fast. When that person notices that their creative light isn't shining somewhere they just shine it there. Immediate course correction. No self-criticism is necessary because the small, made-up egoic self is not a player here. Not even on the roster.

So there's no thought about the constraints and limits of "my personality" to stop you because you know it's a made-up thing to begin with, and not related to the energy of spirit. Therefore you just move the love light to where you want it to go.

If Christopher were living in the awareness that he was loving, creative energy, he'd just call his sister. The moment he noticed he hadn't talked to her in a long time he would call. Because he wanted his relationship with his sister to grow, he'd shine his creative light in the direction of his sister.

Just as when you notice that your house plant isn't getting any sunlight, you just move it into the light. You don't waste time worrying about what kind of a person you must be to have neglected your plant. You don't try to figure that out before you move the plant. The only thing missing in this (or any) situation is the light.

When an aware person (someone who knows and realizes that they are creative energy itself) notices that the sales of their services have been neglected—resulting in lower income—they simply turn their light (creative energy) toward the sales process.

"Whatever you give your attention to grows" is not just some positive slogan—it's how the world actually works.

The more you become aware that you are infinite, creative energy, the more you can see yourself as light.

Think of it the way a gardener uses a "grow light."

Sometimes called a "plant light," grow lights make it easy to grow plants indoors. Grow lights are used for horticulture, indoor gardening, indoor hydroponics and aquatic plants. Shine a grow light on your indoor plant and you ignite enough photosynthesis for the plant to grow.

Creativity is just like that light. You can shine your grow light anywhere. On your business, on relationships, on your exercise routine, on your music, and on your education.

And the gospel song sings, "This little light of mine, I'm going to let it shine."

You think that if you open up to love, you'll lose your independence or your self-expression or creativity or whatever you call all that passionate, wonderful stuff that makes you feel alive inside.

~ Tom Robbins

Who's doing the creating?

Most people I know who struggle with performing well in business or personal life think the answer lies somewhere inside the question of "Who am I?" They don't see that the real answer lies in the question, "*What* am I?"

Because when the answer to the "what" question arises as "pure, loving, creative energy," you only need to choose where you want to direct that.

If, however, as is the case for most people, you keep going to "Who am I?" you'll get lost in trying to decide how you should judge and label yourself today. Are you an introvert, a lazy person, a "3" on the enneagram, a Pisces, a coward, a detail person, a daydreamer, a fool, a . . . who in the hell?

You keep doing that and meanwhile the plant you wanted to grow dies. Your good work dies. What you want to create never gets created.

But only because you're looking in the wrong place. You're going personal with everything. Shrinking everything down to the ego. Where there's no light at all.

And why do you do that?

You do it because everyone else does it. We all do it because we have agreed that we are each very personal entities . . . and covered with labels.

Actually these mistaken identities may even start out as fun! It can feel like fun when we're gossiping, judging and labeling and praising and criticizing others and, eventually, ourselves. But if you're like me you will end up (in the words of the novelist John Barth) lost in the funhouse.

The alternative to being lost in the funhouse is to actually live as creativity itself. Divine, loving creative energy. The light. To be it. Not to try to figure out whether you are creative, or how creative you are, or to compare yourself to people who seem to be more creative than you, but to be it and live it. Knowing that it's what you are and all you are.

It's all anybody is.

There is no ranking system. No leaderboard.

When we're all swimming in the ocean, no one asks, "Who's more in the ocean?"

There are two points of view. Both are normal, one is true. From the point of view of a personal or separate self, there are distinct objects, events, and selves. There is isolation; only insecurity. From the point of view of Consciousness itself, there is one indivisible, yet perpetually changing experience. There is freedom; only Love.

~ Garret Kramer

Not taking this gift personally

Creative energy is anything but personal.

It's bigger than that. Which is why artists, poets, inventors and musical composers so often say they have no idea where their best ideas came from. It certainly doesn't feel like they are the result of personal thinking, or of their proud ego "figuring it out." They often say the work "came through me" from somewhere.

Bob Dylan hadn't given an interview in nineteen years when he sat down with Ed Bradley in 2004 on *60 Minutes*.

Bradley asked him where his song ideas and great lyrics came from.

Dylan said, "I don't know how I got to write those songs."

"What do you mean you don't know how?" said Bradley.

Dylan said, "All those early songs were almost magically written."

Bradley stared at him and Dylan paused and then began to recite some of his song lyrics. He said, "Darkness at the break of noon, shadows even the silver spoon, a handmade blade, the child's balloon . . ."

He paused and looked at Bradley and then said. "Well, try to sit down and write something like that."

Later in the interview Bradley asked him how he wrote his famous song "Blowin' In The Wind." Dylan said only that it came out of "that wellspring of creativity." He said he probably wrote the song in a matter of minutes.

I noticed that there was no talk from Dylan of "*my* creativity" or "*my* system" or "*my* unique talent."

It was *the* wellspring.

We all have it. In fact, it's all we have. We just use it differently, depending on our levels of consciousness and awareness, and depending on what we choose to practice creating.

The recollection of how, when and where it all happened became vague as the lingering strains hung in the rafters of the studio. I wanted to shout back at it, "Maybe I didn't write you, but I found you."

~ **Hoagy Carmichael**

The light of time and attention

Once I was writing a book whose basic subject was fear. It was an unusual challenge for someone like me whose early life story seemed to have been jerked along by one act of cowardice after another.

So I called the most creative person I knew for advice. And, yes, I know we are all wellsprings of infinite creativity, but some of us have been able to create more beautifully and powerfully than others, for whatever reason. And my friend Fred Knipe was one of those people.

I'd had the great fortune and fun to write songs for a living for a number of years and the only reason that worked out was the fact that Fred was my co-writer. He also wrote many songs on his own, and he'd won Emmys for his TV screenwriting and made a good living as a comedian as well. No one in my life had such a great track record of converting his innate creativity into amazing creations for people to enjoy.

So getting his advice on how to write that book was an obvious move on my part.

I asked him, "What's the most important factor in making sure this book is all it can be? I really want this to be a great book. What's the one thing that will make it great?"

His answer surprised me.

I'd expected him to give me some kind of magical algorithm or secret sauce that only a creative genius would know about. I was prepared to take notes on it and ask him questions about it so that I wouldn't misunderstand the nuances of it. I wanted to learn this most important factor and apply it to my book.

So what was it? His simple answer was, "Time spent with the book."

What?

That sounded so simple and ordinary. Blue collar, even. Where was the magic in that? Where were the magical nuances I longed for?

I immediately thought about all those stories about creative flashes of genius arriving to artists, writers and inventors in mere seconds. Didn't Bob Dylan tell Ed Bradley that "Blowin' in the Wind" was written in a matter of minutes? Don't we all have infinite, loving creative energy at our fingertips?

But the longer I reflected on his answer, the more I saw it. We do have access to infinite creativity. All of us do. But when it comes to creating something big and exciting, there's more to it.

So Fred's advice—"time spent with the book"—hit me like a silver hammer and has stayed with me ever since.

I've since learned that most great creative work usually depends deeply on **time and attention**. And time and attention are usually overlooked. Nobody seems to realize that time and attention are the *true* secret sauces.

For creating anything.

Because even Dylan's song, which seemed to come so quickly, was preceded by the years of time and attention he gave to writing his earlier songs, and to the deep study of poetry, blues, popular ballads and folk music that he had done. Not just casually, but thoroughly and obsessively.

The artist Pablo Picasso is best known for the wildly unconventional paintings he did late in his life. We might assume he just opened his channel to the infinite and let the shapes and colors fly! And perhaps he did. But the younger Picasso also received great discipline and training from his father, and then later from the more traditional academies of art in which he trained.

When writing about Picasso in *The Zen of Creativity*, American Zen master John Daido Loori pointed out, "Originality is born of craftsmanship, skill and diligent practice, not from trying to stand out in a crowd."

So creativity is our infinite nature, *and* extraordinary creative works thrive on the gift of time and attention.

And although that sounds like ordinary blue-collar work ethic, it's actually the secret portal to creating something wonderful. It delivers the one thing people don't think they have: internal, reliable access!

Because we can't just "do" the magic of a flash of creative insight on command. We have to wait for that. Allow it in rather than force it to happen.

But we *can* do time and attention. All of us can. And the more we do that, the more often the insights come.

If someone buys me a hundred spins of the roulette wheel, my likelihood of winning money goes way up. Even though I will never know ahead of time which exact spin will be a winner for me.

Most people leave the wheel after a single spin. Or two.

"That didn't work. It's not my thing. It's not me. My sister is creative but I'm obviously not."

Most people embarking on a creative project, like a book, or a song or a painting or an innovative advertising campaign take one (or two) spins and then back away from the table.

No instant gratification? No immediate cause and effect? Then I'm out. It must be magic, this creativity thing, and I don't seem to have it.

After my talk with Fred Knipe (and you can find some of his creative works in the *Resources* section at the end of the book) I began to see how time and attention were often the great missing pieces in *whatever* someone was trying to create—great or small, extraordinary or ordinary.

If I noticed that an online course I was teaching didn't have many students enrolled in it yet, I would look at my calendar and see that I hadn't given enrollment into the school very much time and attention yet. So I would then block out longer calendar spaces in the coming days and weeks to apply my attention to enrollment.

Whatever you shine that light on grows and flourishes. Flowers teach us that. The garden teaches us all we need to know about flourishing as a creator.

I soon began to see Fred's wisdom in my work as a coach and consultant. I even began to see that almost all my clients' and colleagues' **"How do I . . .?"** questions could be usefully answered with "Time and attention."

"I'm nervous about a talk I have to give . . . *how do I* make these nerves go away?"

Would you be willing to give the preparation and rehearsal of your talk more time and attention?

"Okay, yeah, I could do that."

Later I would hear, "That advice you gave me was amazing! How do you know that stuff?"

I might say, "Years of experience." But if I were more honest, I'd have said, "I now always say '*time and attention*' whenever anyone asks for a solution."

Because time and attention give creativity a chance to show

up for you. Otherwise you are too continuously distracted and interrupted by things you are reacting to all day. Your inherent creativity doesn't have an opportunity to show you what it can do.

"How do I create a better relationship with my teenage daughter?"

How much time and attention does she receive from you? Does she feel heard by you? Understood? Loved? Even liked? Does she experience you as someone who likes spending time with her?

Time and attention are what shine your creative light on the rich, damp soil of your garden. Yet people don't see it. (Just like I didn't see it when I called Fred.) They walk right past it. They want something more exotic. Maybe something that contains an unusual and startling trick, a hidden move, maybe something from the ancient wisdom of China, or something only Google software designers know about. Something that resembles an elegant karate kick to the throat of the opponent. Something super cool that can be swiftly applied to the problem. Something heretofore unknown to the ordinary person.

But, really. Why even look for that? It's just not there. Why not slow down, clear the deck of distractions, and apply time and attention? Try this for yourself. You say you want a revolution, well here it is.

Again, the great thing about time and attention is that they are something anyone can apply. They are something you and I can always do. And the great thing is that they take the mystery out of initiating the creative process.

Most people block their own potential for creative acts by making the whole idea mysterious. They soon come to believe that extraordinary creativity is awesome . . . but unreachable.

When I was writing song lyrics for a living I used to sit at my desk and wonder, "Where do people's great ideas come from? I don't know! *They* don't even know! So I'll just hope I get one once in a while."

Meanwhile I'd go back to being a reactor, fighting the good fight against circumstance. Soon I was equating my life in the music business with impending doom.

I'm always able to see extreme "creativity" in other people, people like Lin-Manuel Miranda! Or Georgia O'Keefe! Or Grace VanderWaal or Drake or my friend who painted a mural at her church! But by comparing myself to them every time I see their work, I distance myself from creativity itself.

And in doing so, I distance myself from my true nature.

And we all do that until we don't.

Let the space
in which
your thoughts appear
and the space
in which
the world appears
find each other

~ Rupert Spira

Just find your path

Personalizing my explanation for why I'm not creating what I want to create has always turned out to be the wrong way to go for me.

Anytime I collapsed into "What is it about me?" creativity would disappear.

That was my hardest lesson: learning that creativity isn't personal. The creative flow is not related to the ego. No matter how much the ego tries to get involved and take credit.

I also used to think I had to *force* creativity to happen. When I was writing song lyrics for a living I used to sit over my typewriter and bang my head with my fist, trying to force creativity.

It was only after I gave up, pushed my chair back, and heaved a big self-pitying sigh that the words would start to appear . . . they would appear like fireflies in the dark night . . . and soon I could begin to see them.

A friend recently asked me for help. She said, "I find myself switching back and forth between things and not really creating my career. Once I hit a snag I am tempted to stop or switch to something else. How did you solve this?" I thought for a long time. Then it hit me. This isn't about some personal problem that has to be solved. It's more about a direction. In other words:

There is a path.

A path to the completion of what you want to create.

A new song? A freshly painted bedroom? The ability to play "Over the Rainbow" on the ukulele? The creation of a prosperous career? Whatever you want to create!

There is a path.

And when you're not on that path you're not creating, and when you are on the path you're making progress.

Sometimes I hit a snag and am tempted to leave the path for a while. Sometimes I do leave and walk down a side road.

But the path is always there. It waits for me. It has no judgment. It will wait days, months and even years for me.

You asked, "How did you solve this?"

There was nothing to solve. Because there was no real problem. There was only (but always) a path. A path you were not on. And the good news is that a path is not a problem.

It's something you're on or you're not.

If I see that I've left the path for too long to do something else, I can just go back to the path. If I want to create what the path leads to, I know to go back to the path.

I'm not going to hang out with celebrities, I'm not going to parties. I have two songs due for *Moana* next week, and I'm going to go and spend some time with Maui and Moana in the ocean, in my mind.

~ Lin-Manuel Miranda

Rommel, You Magnificent Bastard

In the movie *Patton*, there is an unforgettable scene in which George C. Scott, playing the role of General George S. Patton, has just spent weeks studying the writing of his Nazi adversary, Field Marshall Erwin Rommel.

Patton is winning a ferocious tank battle against Rommel's forces in Tunisia and is looking out over the battlefield through binoculars. In deep admiration for his enemy's efforts, he says, "Rommel, you magnificent bastard. I read your book!"

Patton is demonstrating how effective it is to learn from people we admire, instead of distancing ourselves by comparing ourselves unfavorably.

Great artists and musicians love to incorporate the work of others into their own work. Whether they are doing it consciously or subconsciously. They see something more advanced than their own work, and rather than shrinking down from it, they embrace it and take it in. Instead of thinking, "How does this make little ole me feel?" they get excited and ask, "How can I use this?"

Most people—almost all people—spend their days comparing themselves unfavorably to people. I know I did, for many decades.

Why do we do this? Is it because we don't understand

creativity and its source?

We are its source!

I remember being seven years old and drawing airplanes and cars in class while the teacher was trying to teach something uninteresting. When I looked at the boy next to me who was also drawing airplanes, I saw that his were *so much* better than mine. I became discouraged and stopped drawing.

This is why so many people say, "I can't sing" or "I can't draw" or "I can't dance." Even though when they were younger they had no such thoughts and were happy to dance and sing or draw any time they had a chance to.

But over time, due to their new socially-encouraged habit of COMPARING, they dropped out of creating.

Clients I work with today do subtle versions of the same thing. They observe someone more successful than they are in their field and they recoil into a little ball.

Or they back away from the canvas. They feel inferior. Inferiority soon becomes a complex.

But when someone somehow retains full connection to their God-given, always-present, divine and loving creativity they don't compare. If they see something inspiring, they incorporate. They integrate.

An enthusiastic young basketball player shows me his moves on the playground and yells out, "I got this from Michael Jordan! I got this from Steph Curry! This is the turnaround drive I learned from LeBron!"

Elvis Presley used to study the singing styles of gospel singers and rhythm and blues stars. In his era, southern white singers were not even thinking of doing that. Elvis used to watch soul singers Jackie Wilson and James Brown on television and thrill to their dance moves. You can find their moves in Elvis' moves, just as you can find many of Elvis' moves in Mick Jagger's and so on. Musicians and singers call them "influences" and they are proud to talk about them.

The average person would think of doing this as "stealing" or "copying," which are socially unacceptable activities, and this is why the average person is no longer a creator. Even though they were born to create. They have replaced creating with mild social anxiety. They learn to live as a reactor, even though they admire the creators they see. They're also intimidated by the creativity they see.

My grandson Jude visited us recently. He was a year and a half old. When he saw me playing the piano, he lit up. He came up to the piano and started "playing it" right along with me, a big smile on his face. Not yet talked out of expressing his own natural creative energy, he saw a piano being played and immediately heard a voice inside him that said, "I can do that!" He does that everywhere he goes. He sees his mother doing laundry and he picks up some laundry thinking, "I can do that!" He sees her cooking on the stove and he reaches up to turn up the heat dial on the stove because he thinks, "I can do that!"

That same "can do" spirit is in all of us. We're born with it. It's our natural confidence. It isn't the adult version (or, story about) confidence which says it has to be built up and developed over time.

Elvis never disconnected from his child-like creativity. He saw Jackie Wilson and said, "I can do that!" Freddie Mercury was the same way.

We only call it "child-like" because we see it in children. But it's in all of us, always there, right up to our last breath.

I was once on an airline flight seated next to the great jazz guitarist and singer George Benson. I thought I recognized him, and then when I looked down at the boarding pass he'd set down between our seats I saw his name.

It was a real thrill for me to talk to him during the flight and listen to his great stories and opinions. He told me that when he does his concerts he notices that aspiring guitar players often sit in the front seats over to his left so they can steal his riffs and runs as his fingers go up and down the neck of the guitar. He laughed when he said, "When I get to my new stuff, my best stuff, I can see their necks craning so they can see it and steal it, so I turn my guitar at that moment so it's out of their view. It drives them crazy."

We both laughed at that. But when I thought about it later I realized how joyful and widespread this act of "theft" can be in the world of creativity.

When the brilliant and crazy gonzo journalist/author Hunter Thompson was starting out as a writer he used to sit down and copy Ernest Hemingway's books. He'd write the whole Hemingway book out sentence by sentence, word for word. Just to get that sparse, impactful cadence and style programmed into his brain. He wasn't reading Hemingway and thinking, "I can't do that. I'll never be as good as Hemingway. I might as well give up."

Instead, he saw what he loved and jumped all over it. He incorporated it. He mixed it in.

There is something better in this than mere impersonation. Did Elvis look exactly like Jackie Wilson when he did his moves on stage? Did Hunter Thompson's writing read exactly like Hemingway's? Not at all! Because they weren't just mimicking. They weren't just straight-out copying. They were integrating. They were making it their own.

In a televised interview with Dan Rather, pop singer Michael Bublé was asked about his influences as a singer. He then did amazing impressions of Frank Sinatra, Elvis Presley and Dean Martin. You can hear those singers in the way Bublé sings today, even though Bublé has his own unique and captivating sound.

These acts of joyful integration and incorporation done by musicians and artists and athletes are available to average people like you and me. If only we could see it. If only we would not make everything so self-consciously personal.

When my life was nothing but personal, and I was doing nothing but comparing myself to others (unfavorably) I would go listen to a friend give a talk to a group of people and hear how entertaining and powerful the talk was and say to myself, "Wow. I can't do that." That was my automatic thought about anything and anyone I admired. I was making everything personal and always thinking, "That's not me."

But when I began to see that nothing had to be personal, and everything could be creative, I could hear the same kind of talk and think, "Oh yes, I do love this. I am getting so many ideas from this! This is beautiful. I am going to use a version of this!"

My speaker friend might see the happy look on my face as we talk after his presentation. He might ask me what I was thinking and I would say, "I was thinking, *Rommel, you magnificent bastard.*"

With a little more care, a little more courage, and, above all, a little more soul, our lives can be so easily discovered and celebrated in work, and not, as now, squandered and lost in its shadow.

~ David Whyte

This energy is who you are

This creative energy is who you are.

And when I say things like "who you are" it's not really me condescendingly telling you something you should know. It's not something I'm demonstrating superior knowledge of. I need to hear it as much as you do. I can get as much from these words as you can. When I write them or speak them I'm reminding me of something I will all too often forget.

Creativity is flowing energy. It's not a static, frozen thing.

And it doesn't belong to the ego.

The ego wants it. But it really just wants the label of it: "He's creative!" But creativity comes from beyond the ego. It springs from an intelligent energy always present. Beyond my personal thinking. Beyond my tiny ego.

Creativity is also fun. When I use it to create something, the fun increases. For example, it's really fun to create a new skill.

Most people think skill is an outgrowth from inherent talent. A thing produced by a thing.

The linear, logical, personal-thinking mind has a real thing for things. It wants every phenomenon and every experience to be caused by a thing. That's why it doesn't know how to understand and dissolve into pure energy, because energy is movement . . . moving too fast and free to paste a label on it.

It doesn't see that energy and creativity are the same, in that there's is no "thing" involved. There is only movement. There is a flowing, spiraling, pouring-out, expanding, progressing movement. A busting out! When the obstacles to creativity are removed, it pours forth on its own. The ego doesn't do it or control it.

It's much like the month of June in Michigan. All the new green leaves and yellow flowers and once-frozen rivers are now flowing out and flourishing. If you don't know what creativity is, if you can't put your finger on it, come to Michigan in June. June will be, like the song says, "bustin' out all over." You'll see yourself, if you look closely enough.

Skills are not things that come from things, as people want to believe. They have to believe that to keep their thing-world-picture in place.

So, for example, if an American ambassador to France speaks perfect French at a dinner party in Paris, her husband might smile proudly and say to the guest next to him, "She was always good with language. She always had that skill."

"Do you speak French too?"

"Oh my, no! No, no, no. Not me. No, that's a skill I wasn't born with. Not my thing."

In his mind, that skill is a thing. Speak French? No way. A practically unattainable thing! French is like Greek to him.

He is unaware . . . unmindful . . . and unappreciative of his inborn, ever-present, creativity. He doesn't see that his wife *created* her ability to speak French. From nothing. She created a path for learning, stayed on the path, and now speaks fluently. Fluently! It's a flourishing! She used the same creativity that he has but doesn't know he has because he's hung up on explaining his world as a collection of permanent things. You either have them or you don't.

His wife is actually unusual. Most American ambassadors do not speak the language of the country they are ambassadors to. Why is that? Well, when you ask them they probably say they are "not good with languages." That skill is a thing they unfortunately don't have.

That's their belief. In other words, that's their superstition. Which is to say, that's their ignorance. That's their story, made up out of nothing and seasoned with psychological mythology, cultural superstition and personal fear.

You notice, if you listen to him long enough, that our typical American ambassador speaks English. Long into the night! A rapturous, expressive, voluminous, bawdy English. So many funny stories. Such great metaphors! You have to look twice at him to make sure he's not Scott Fitzgerald!

But wait. What was that he said earlier? He said he was not good with languages. Yet this English that he showers on us with such flair and fluency was actually learned by him when he was a child!

So what's going on here? How could he learn it as a child? Was he some kind of child-genius with languages who later in life suffered a DNA-destroying injury? Was he suddenly intellectually damaged and turned into a person who no longer had this thing (he calls a skill) known as "good with languages"?

No.

What's happening with him is the result of a trade he has unconsciously made. He has exchanged his beautiful reality (infinite creativity) for an illusion. A superstition. A story about himself. A story built from limitations. He's shut off his innate, God-given creative energy and traded it for a personality.

Now he thinks he's a permanent person. A thing! A hard object. A marble statue of himself. He has frozen his creative energy into an imaginary thing.

We can criticize him for "not caring enough" or "not having the commitment" to learn French and be the best ambassador he can be. We can call him an arrogant, clueless, privileged American.

But then we're doing the same thing to him as he's doing to himself. We're making him into a permanent thing with our judgment of him. We're not seeing him as divine, creative energy. We've become as clueless as he is.

Which is a great thing to see when you see it. Isn't it?

Do you see it? If you do, then the next question can be, "Where's *my* next language? What rich and glorious new skill would I like to be fluent in?"

And "fluent" is the word.

My dictionary says the word "fluent" comes from "the Latin word *fluere*, meaning 'to flow,' which gives us the root *flu*."

Words from the Latin *fluere* have something to do with flowing. A *fluid* is a substance that flows . . . When someone is *fluent* in a language the words flow out of her or him.

You can put anything you want into that flow.

There is something deeper than this "I" thought, and all other thoughts. That is truly who I am. There is a conscious, alive, intelligent, loving beingness here in this moment, watching all these thoughts arise.

~ Scott Kiloby

Oh, no, not your name

My friend was hurting. He was going through a divorce and his ex-wife was continuously angry.

And worse, there were children involved, and when my friend went to his ex's home to pick up or drop off the children, she and he would argue.

The arguments didn't stop there. She would call him to continue the arguments. He'd be going through his day, his phone would buzz, and he'd look down to see her name. Oh no. Not her.

Thoughts would swirl in his head and his heart would sink and his anxiety would rise before he finally was braced enough to answer.

"What now?"

So you can see that the anxiety and upset went both ways.

Then one day he got an idea.

He thought back to his times a year or so ago when he felt so good. He was in a recovery program that had completely turned his life around. One of the exercises recommended in the program was to identify your resentments and, when you are ready and willing, send a prayer for the person you resent.

It was much like the transformative Metta meditation taught

in Buddhism, where you wish for (and send in the form of light) happiness, health and well-being to people, even those who have mistreated you.

My friend recalled the power he felt working his recovery program, and inside that feeling he received a creative idea.

He went into his phone and changed his ex-wife's name. So when she called and he looked down to see the name of who was calling he would no longer see her name and every stressful thing he associated with it. Instead, when she called and he looked down at his phone, he would see the words he replaced her name with: "Pray for Her."

It changed everything.

I thought about that story many times after he told it to me. I thought about it on many levels. On one commonplace level, it was just a clever little trick to snap him out of a bad feeling.

But looking deeper I saw it as a courageous act of creativity.

On the shallower level one might say he was coming up with a good way not to be triggered by the sight of her name.

But it was better than that.

And maybe the best way I can explain that is to highlight the phrase "triggered by." This is a very popular phrase, even in spiritual circles. When I was teaching a graduate class at the University of Santa Monica, a school for spiritual psychology, many of the students (full graduates of the University) would talk to me during the breaks in the lecture hall or after class and tell me about the things they were "triggered by."

Some said they were triggered by certain people, or things people said to them, or even particular words I had used when I taught. When I asked what they actually meant by "triggered by" they told me that those things (words and people) caused them to feel anxiety, stress or even anger and fear.

Well, hold on. Your university and its founders teach a

psychological principle called "I'm upset because . . ." And what that means is if you put anything outside of you after the word "because" you've got it wrong. In other words, people, places, things, events and situations cannot be the direct cause of your upset. (No matter that 95 percent of people believe otherwise. That's only 95 percent. It used to be that 100 percent of people believed the world was flat.)

How does this relate to my friend creating "Pray for Her?"

Well, because most people would think he was being triggered by her name. And that would mean that her name, and by extension she herself, were causing bad feelings in him. Triggering those feelings in him. Causing them. Directly.

Not how the brain works.

The brain is better than that. Life is better than that. We are creators. And even when it feels like we are reactors, we are only reacting to our own creations!

So when her name comes up, it doesn't cause any feelings. It can't. My mind has to create (and it does so lightning-fast, in nanoseconds) a thought about that name, then a story around that thought, for me to feel anything associated with that name of hers.

Fortunately my friend already knew this. But what if he hadn't? What if he was one of those people who believes in triggers? Well, he could check it out if he was in an exploratory mood.

Let's say he wanted to find out if the name itself was causing him to feel stressed. When she called, and her name came up, he could show the name to people around him at work, people who didn't know her name. He could hold out the phone when it buzzed and show it to the person in the seat next to him at the staff meeting. She would look at it and then look back up at him with a questioning face.

"What?" she would say.

"Look!" he'd say.

"Okay, what? Someone's calling you."

He might then say to her, "How does it make you feel? Seeing that name?"

"Well, nothing. Should I feel something?"

Now his exploration would get interesting. Because no matter how many people he showed her name to, he would find out that her name is not doing any triggering.

At least not to people that haven't created a story around it.

Bingo.

So that might lead him back to the story, built around his own thought, as the source of what he feels. The cause. Wow. He's found it! It's inside him. It's not out there.

Some spiritual teachers and psychologists explain this discovery by using the metaphor of the projector versus the camera. We've been taught to think the mind is a camera, recording and taking in things from the outside, including triggers. But upon further and deeper exploration we discover it's more like a film projector, with the light of consciousness shining through the film of thought and projecting it out upon the external world.

That's a creative process.

No thought has any power. You have power. And when you identify and believe in the thought you give power to the thought.

~ **Mooji**

How I block creativity's flow

The fastest way I block creativity from flowing through me and into the world is with a characteristic.

In the game of life, if I want to block my own creativity, I place a piece on the board called a characteristic. In other words, a label. For example, if I'm about to reach out to someone I want to do business with, I might put a piece on the board to block myself, saying, "INTROVERT to block."

That's because I think I'm an introvert. It's a label that means I'm inherently shy, so I don't reach out. The ability to reach out remains on the side of the game board. An option? Not a direct option, because I've blocked it with "INTROVERT." So far, anyway. Maybe I can do some more generalized marketing and advertising that my prospective client might accidentally see. Sure, it will cost a lot of money. And whether my prospect will even see it is a long shot.

I'm not able to see that I could have used another "option" piece: I could have created a conversation with the person. If I hadn't blocked it with a characteristic . . . some label I put on myself.

What's ironic and even amusing once I see it is that this permanent individual person, the player, me, made up of characteristics and labels, was a creation. It was made up. It was created so devotedly and thoroughly that it was made to look real.

The irony is that I used unlimited creativity to create a permanent identity that now limits creativity. Like the story of God dreaming up Satan. Like "the good book" filled with "good news" dreaming up the anti-Christ.

Today I have clients who have done the same thing as I did. They tell me what they are not good at. I ask them why they think they're not good at it, and they say, in effect, that it's simply because they're not good at it.

I pressed a business leader recently who'd just been promoted to his first leadership position about why he thought he wasn't good at leading meetings.

"I'm not wired that way," he said.

I asked him if he'd asked for help. Maybe there was someone in the company who he thought was good at leading meetings. Maybe they could help him learn.

He said, "I'm not good at asking for help."

Characteristic to block, characteristic to block. (Permanent self to imprison.)

Then I asked him if he spoke French.

"No."

"Why not?"

"Well, I don't speak French."

"Why do you think that is?"

He was puzzled. He said, "Well I don't speak French because I haven't taken the time to learn French and practice French."

Oh, good! Somewhere, deep down, he gets it. I was afraid he was going to say he was hardwired to speak English. But with something simple, impersonal and non-threatening like a language, he sees how it *all* works.

I asked him to consider the possibility that he was not good at leading meetings because, like French, he hasn't taken the time to learn and practice leading meetings. And the reason he thought he wasn't good at asking for help was simply because, over the years, he has not yet practiced asking for help.

The permanent, characteristic-bound personality he has created blocks the creation of new skills, new powers, new possibilities.

It does that for him, and it does that for all of us whenever we fall for the illusion of personal permanence.

Therefore, to reactivate our awareness of infinite creativity, we might want to replace every "I'm not good at" with "I have not given time and attention to the practice of that."

With that awareness, we can create almost anything.

You can't use up creativity.
The more you use,
the more you have.

~ **Maya Angelou**

How I flunked journaling class

So many people told me over the years that keeping a gratitude journal was a great and useful thing to do that I thought I needed to give it a try.

That was back in the day when I believed my happiness and sense of fulfillment were dependent on lots of stuff out there in the world, outside of me. Things! Things like cars, houses, musical instruments, books, sound systems, jobs, money, friends and lovers. Just to get started.

So the chase for accumulation was always on. My feelings of unhappiness and anxiety drove me to try to add more objects of desire. For most of them the pleasure charge didn't last, so they'd always have to be upgraded or replaced.

The continuous seeking became a dangerous, high-speed chase, because it seemed like I never could go fast enough and obtain enough things or relationships to make me feel at peace. I knew I needed more, and I always hoped that certainly someday, if I chased hard enough, I'd *have it*.

Therefore I was always looking for something that would help me go faster toward this eventual fulfillment. Any self-improvement trick or technique you might suggest would be worth a try.

One day a friend recommended I keep a gratitude journal. When I questioned the practical value of that he sent me a quote from Deepak Chopra, who said, "Gratitude opens the door to . . . the power, the wisdom, the creativity of the universe."

Power, wisdom and creativity? Really? That would make it worth a try. Those three things would certainly help me get what I wanted faster. So I was in. I'd see if keeping this journal would give my mission for acquisition a measurable boost.

So I began to keep a gratitude journal. I would wake up in the morning and list the things I was grateful for. It was hard to think of things at first, but I finally was able to find things to put on my list. As the days went by, I wasn't noticing any increases in power, wisdom and creativity, but I was willing to hang in there. Maybe it would take a while.

But then something discouraging began to happen. As the weeks went by I noticed that my gratitude list was getting smaller! That was weird. Was this supposed to happen?

Some of the people I'd had on the list had let me down so I took them off. The car I'd been listing was falling apart so it came off. My sound system didn't work right any more so it came off the list, too. My family didn't appreciate me at a gathering I went to so I took the lot of them off. One day both of my dogs wouldn't stop barking so they came off the list.

The smaller my list got, the more useless the whole thing felt.

So I stopped keeping the journal. I even threw the little notebook itself away so I wouldn't have to see it and have it remind me of the latest failed project.

Looking back from this vantage point now, I can see what my problem was. I was only trying to find gratitude for *things*. They were all things that come and go. And even when they seemed to stay, their ability to "make me happy" always wore down. So they went off the list. How can you be grateful for something that no longer makes you happy?

If you had asked me back then why the things on my list were not making me happy I would have said, "Because they're not enough!"

So what, then, did I actually want? Back then I might have said, "I want it all."

Even though I had no idea what that meant. But it sounded like it would do the trick. It sounded like a bold mission. And I noticed that people were often admired for raising a fist and saying, "I want it all!"

Salespeople and self-improvement marketers seemed to love people who said that. They encouraged that goal and said things like, "Yeah, baby, say yes to your badass self! We're gonna help you go out there and crush it! You deserve to have it all!"

I tried to get myself to believe my badass self deserved to have it all, but it was never something I could take seriously.

Today I see many badass people keeping gratitude journals that contain the same kinds of lists of shiny objects that I tried to accumulate. They list all the people, places and things they hope someday will reach critical mass, that final tipping point that replaces "I'm not enough" with "Now I have it all."

If these people are anything like I was, their journals have the wrong stuff in them. Yes, it's unfairly judgmental to use the word "wrong." But it's in the same spirit that I would tell you that your flashlight had the wrong kind of battery in it and that's why it gives no light.

What should I put in my journal?

If you want it to give light, why not look to the source of all creativity and put *that* in your gratitude journal. Instead of all those outside things that have already been created by others.

And if you really opened up to that source, you probably

wouldn't need a whole journal for it. You could use a post-it note or a drink coaster at the bar. You could just write the word "consciousness," and there's your whole gratitude list right there.

But who would really do that? Who would wake up and put "consciousness" as the only thing in their gratitude journal? Who today even puts it in as *one* of the things? If we could seize and read all the gratitude journals being kept in the world today we probably wouldn't find it listed anywhere. Too bad we don't yet have Gratitude Police to do that.

Who among the keepers of journals realizes at the deepest level of appreciation that without consciousness there would be nothing, not even their little journal? No journal and certainly nothing to put in it.

But if that were to change for you and me?

What if consciousness itself were deeply appreciated first thing each day? What if that overwhelming feeling of gratitude had us waking up and "falling in love with awareness," as the spiritual philosopher Greg Goode puts it?

I bet that would have us hearing the words differently when Deepak Chopra says, "Gratitude opens the door to . . . the power, the wisdom, the creativity of the universe." My guess is that Chopra himself, when recommending gratitude, was not referring to the little material things we are putting into our gratitude journals. As his book *You Are the Universe* suggests, we can go bigger than that.

Once my primary gratitude at the deepest level of the heart became gratitude for life itself and the conscious awareness that is behind it all, it no longer became necessary to use a journal to jump-start that feeling.

But there's a big "however" here. An important counterpoint.

Because even though it helped me make a point to say that most people put the "wrong" stuff in their journals, I do know many people who keep these kinds of journals and benefit greatly from them. It helps them develop their feeling and expression of gratitude.

As those feelings grow through cultivation, they find themselves adding more and more things to the journal. Even formerly inconsequential and problematic things start to get added. Even people they see as difficult people start to get added to the journal!

These kinds of journal-keepers are different than I was. They see more than I did. Their hearts are more open than mine was. Their judgments fall away, and their appreciation for impermanence and the transparency of things grows each day. Soon their journals are open to including everything. Everything they are conscious of.

That's when they see that they no longer need to "want it all." Because as one look at their gratitude list tells them—they already have it all.

The more you trust and rely upon the Spirit, the greater your capacity to create.

~ **Dieter Uchtdorf**

Herbie Hancock and Miles Davis

We love following "creative people"—people who express their creativity so gloriously—because they return us to what we are made of. They bring us home. They delight us with a creativity that connects.

Connects with what?

With itself.

In us.

And although my whole point in this book is to remind you (and me) that we ourselves have the same infinite creativity that "creative people" have, it is also true that there are people who have found and developed ways to express it more dramatically than the rest of us.

Which is why we love them.

People like Herbie Hancock and Miles Davis. Hancock is a popular jazz pianist, keyboardist, bandleader, and composer. And Miles Davis was a legendary jazz trumpeter and composer.

Hancock recorded a recent video you can find online in which he talked about his memory of a "hot night" in Stuttgart, when the music was "tight, it was powerful, it was innovative, and fun."

He was playing piano and Miles Davis was on trumpet. Playing behind one of Davis' solos, Hancock hit a wrong chord. It was an embarrassing mistake and Hancock was upset with himself. But only for a split second. Because right then something strange happened.

Miles just went with it.

He played into the chord as if it wasn't wrong at all.

Hancock said, "Miles paused for a second, and then he played some notes that made my chord right... Miles was able to turn something that was wrong into something that was right."

The Persian poet Rumi's famous lines come to mind, "Out beyond right-doing and wrong-doing there is a field. I will meet you there."

Miles Davis met Hancock in that field.

Hancock said, "What I realize now is that Miles didn't hear it as a mistake. He heard it as something that happened. As an event. And so that was part of the reality of what was happening at that moment. And he dealt with it . . . Since he didn't hear it as a mistake, he thought it was his responsibility to find something that fit that moment."

Do I have to be on stage in a jazz band to live this way?

To take what's "wrong" in my life and simply create with it?

I used to give a short seminar to businesses called "Welcoming Every Circumstance." It encouraged my clients to take customer complaints as positive material to create from. They would learn to create new systems, new agreements and newer, more trusting relationships with customers.

Most businesses and people go the other way. They cope with, deal with, block out, solve or overcome whatever is wrong. Their relationship to circumstance is defensive. ("I'm really up against it!!") It ignores creativity. And because that creative flow that wants to flow is repressed and blocked and thwarted, the day is long and filled with stress.

A blocked system will always be stressed.

A personality will suffer. There will be a stress fracture. Just as more awareness of creativity leads to a less stressful life. As the Radiohead lyric says, "Be constructive with your blues."

Any time we want to create something truly new and fresh in the world, we must go beyond the noise of our own mind and into the quiet of the fertile void out of which all things come into being.

~ **Michael Neill**

Every breath we drew was Hallelujah

Even though creative energy is who we are and always there, it's difficult for adults in this culture to give it expression. Certainly not like we did as children.

The same creativity we had as children is still there, ready to sing out, or build out, or dance out, but our ego's worries and fears about survival have boarded up the process.

Like putting boards on our windows and doors that ended up with keeping the hurricane *inside*.

But as we saw, there are those who do allow creativity to break through and channel out. Those people create great things, and we can take inspiration from them.

One of my many inspirations is obviously Leonard Cohen. He has lit me up since I first heard Judy Collins sing his song "Suzanne" decades ago. People are most familiar with his famous song, "Hallelujah." It has been recorded by over a hundred different artists, and it keeps appearing in movies and on TV series and was even a big musical moment in the Olympics when K.D. Lang sang it in the closing ceremony. Few songs have ever had that kind of widespread impact.

One might wonder what kind of dramatic visitation Leonard

Cohen's muse must have made. Some stormy night with flashes of light and inspiration coming in through the bedroom curtains making him sit bolt upright in bed groping frantically for his paper and pen.

Actually it didn't happen that way. That song took Cohen two years to write. He had written more than eighty finished verses to it before he selected the final few.

So much for the myth that a creative masterpiece has to happen in a single *flash* of inspiration downloaded from infinite intelligence into a single human unit's brain. Of course that happens sometimes. And the myth might even be accurate about the source. But if what I'm pointing to here is true, that creativity is *always* there for you, then there's no reason why it can't also flow in gently, during the day . . . Moderately but always reliably for those who've learned to open to it.

And not just open to it. But also willing to participate in its arrival.

It doesn't have to be a special esoteric welcoming ceremony. It can be a blue-collar project. It can appear as a craft or a task or a random act of kindness.

Cohen's workmanlike process for writing songs like "Hallelujah" offered its own form of inspiration to me! I don't have to write the perfect verse or be exceptional in every moment. He wrote eighty verses! Wow. That's blue collar taken to the glorious.

I'll tell myself to put on my famous blue work shirt and get moving.

Natalie Goldberg, Zen teacher of creative writing, had some memorable advice for writers that might be something all of us can use, whether we are writers or not.

Her advice was, "Keep your hands moving."

That's it? Yes it is, yet it's usually the last thing I remember to do.

When I own up to my immobile hands, not only do I remember my grandmother singing in the kitchen and telling me "busy hands are happy hands," but I also start to realize that the actual *doing* of creative things really isn't the problem for me. *Thinking about* doing those things is the only thing in my way. It's always harder to do things ahead of time in my mind than it is right now in the real world.

Before I can discard the verse, I have to write it . . . I can't discard a verse before it is written because it is the writing of the verse that produces whatever delights or interests or facets that are going to catch the light. The cutting of the gem has to be finished before you can see whether it shines.

~ Leonard Cohen

Money in her guitar case

My old habits of thought continue to produce the dread and worry that whatever I create won't *compare* well. Not realizing that none of that is important. Comparing is gratuitous. It's a random act of unkindness to myself.

But what if what I create inspires? Who cares about comparison then?

I was inspired by a street singer the other day. I put money in her guitar case and came away glowing with inspiration. She got to me. She sang, "I Will Always Love You."

Did I think, "She doesn't compare to Whitney Houston." No. And the way she sang from the heart, in the moment, I would bet that she wasn't comparing either.

I have a friend who is part of a small mastermind group I meet with quarterly. We all share ideas and experiences and strength and hope about our profession. My friend is a powerful, successful consultant, speaker and author who changes lives with her work on a daily basis. We are inspired by her.

But she compares.

There are people in the group she compares herself to and she begins feeling a little sad and discouraged. Her creativity starts to go into hiding.

She doesn't see yet that when it comes to knowing you are creating a life of profound service to others (which she is), there's no comparison. No need for it. No sense to it. And those rare (but increasing) times when she's in touch with who she really is? Her face lights up. She knows herself as love and beauty and the divine energy of creativity. And inside that *knowing* there is no possibility of comparison.

But creating to serve others is just one aspect of creating. And not even a necessary one for creativity to bestow its gifts upon you. The more you inhabit your creative energy the more you receive the benefits of creating. You can't keep it from getting better and better. And creating can be wonderful even when it doesn't touch or inspire anyone other than you. Don't trust this to be true. You'll know this by testing it. You won't have to try to believe some belief about it based on nothing.

The more good feelings you experience in creation, the more it will occur to you that joyful expression is what the human system was designed to do. It's set up to do that. All ready to go. The natural you will actually proceed to do that.

Unless you mess with it.

Unless you tinker with the natural process and put stuff into it that doesn't belong there. Extraneous stuff like beliefs of limitation and feelings of permanent personal shortcomings. For full-on celebratory expression of creativity you'll want to investigate those beliefs and feelings and send them back into the emptiness from which they came.

Walt Whitman wrote:

I celebrate myself, and sing myself,
And what I assume you shall assume,
For every atom belonging to me as good belongs to you.

And clearly he wasn't singing and celebrating some

belief-bound, isolated entity called "Walt Whitman." His flow of creative poetry and joyful living came from being awake to, and participating in, a much higher, more inclusive "self"— one whose "every atom" is shared by you, and shared by me.

In 1888 Whitman gave an interview to a college newspaper in New Jersey. They asked him for his advice to young writers, and he told them, among other workaday things, to carry a notebook everywhere and engage in writing like it was a long-term work project.

"Whack away at everything pertaining to literary life," he said. "The mechanical part as well as the rest."

Today, if I'm stuck with what I'm creating, I'll look down at the notebook I now carry everywhere and turn to the page where I've written Natalie Goldberg's words:

"Keep your hands moving."

If you could look inside the heart of any and every single human being, you would fall in love with them completely. If you see the inside as it really is and not as your mind projects it to be, you would be so purely in love with the whole thing.

~ **Mooji**

Just show up for work how about?

But it's not just about writing. Creativity wants to play everywhere. Especially in our day-to-day work. My own work as a business and life coach is an example.

Today I have been doing my consulting work with a young man whose website says he's a "success coach." That means if you want to succeed at something you're not succeeding at, you hire him and he'll help you succeed.

He tells me how badly he is struggling. His wife wants him to go back to work in the big corporation he left (because he hated it) because she worries about the fact that he's not getting many clients and not making much income.

I always used to think the idea of an unsuccessful success coach was funny.

But there's some pain in there, too. Actually a lot of it, I'm noticing. I've decided to give him a scholarship to a school I run. He is almost too grateful. He says that for him, it's "the last house on the block."

So he'll be attending my practice-building school for coaches and consultants. He won't feel so alone anymore. He'll meet a lot of coaches who don't understand why they aren't financially successful yet as coaches, why they haven't "created abundance" in their profession.

Usually the answer to that question is very simple. And the solution to the problem isn't mysterious or even very difficult to bring about. The solution reminds me of Leonard Cohen's blue-collar approach to his songwriting craft.

Just as in the arts there is a myth about creativity arriving in huge, unplanned flashes, in coaching there is a myth that says creating a prosperous practice requires flashes of extraordinary personal courage, that succeeding as a coach takes massive amounts of bravado, self-esteem and bold action. You have to jump waaaay out of your comfort zone every week, dream big and hold your breath and holy freaking GO FOR IT!

Okay . . . but why?

What other profession requires that? If you were to tell a friend that you've chosen to be a certified public accountant would your friend say to you, "Wow! Really? OMG, I hope you have the courage!!!"

Of course not, so why is that necessary with coaching? (Almost every starting coach thinks it is.) Especially when the truth is that coaching is an honorable and useful profession in our society today. That's why it is growing so fast. Each year there are more and more coaches making more and more well-earned money. That doesn't happen if the profession is not useful and legit.

So why all the heart-pounding courage being called upon?

Why do people approach it at the coaching pep rallies like it's some huge, IMPOSSIBLE dream that you have to dig down deep into your soul to make manifest?

I have known of new coaches who start their panicky day with meridian tapping for abundance, deep yogic bellows-breathing for elevated mental states, aroma therapy for valor, and petitionary prayers to the supernatural so that they might be blessed with the exceptional, extraordinary powers they will need to make this impossible dream job work.

Hey, just slow down. See if you can get a hold of yourself.

Do you need to scare yourself to make this profession work out financially? Why would that be true?

My experience says it's not true at all. The coaches I've seen succeed just relax and do their jobs. They do the doable. They learn the simple systems used by other successful coaches. They show up for work each day, just like other people do, and they practice their profession, just like an accountant or a lawyer would do.

Or a tinker or a tailor or a soldier would do.

They are okay feeling like average people having an average day making an average amount of progress each day toward professional strength and prosperity.

Rather than taking a daring leap, they just settle in. From there, the good career gets *created*.

The system is that simple: settle in.

Just like you see the pilot on your commercial airline flight settling in prior to the flight. He or she smiles at you, settles in, shares some easy conversation with the attendants and the co-pilot and then goes through the routine instrument check.

The pilot doesn't walk through the jetway hyperventilating, fingering rosary beads and yelling, "Oh My Dear Lord, I hope I'm up to this! God help me and my family!"

At least we hope not.

So why does the coaching profession seem to require that approach—a superhuman victory over the insurmountable?

Maybe it's because this profession often draws inspiration from motivational speakers and authors who tell inspiring stories of humans who achieve things against all odds. My own books and talks often focus on amazing transformations that people make.

Coaches are drawn to this kind of thing, which is great until they start to believe their own profession requires the same kind of unusual and amazing achievements.

Becoming a well-paid professional coach simply doesn't require that.

When a new coach believes that success in this field demands some kind of bravery and extreme daring they have a hard time getting their career off the ground. In fact, they have a hard time looking forward to the next day's work.

How could you consistently look forward to a day of you trying to overcome your fears?

Soon there's no enthusiasm in that coach's day. And that leads to low energy and dwindling access to creativity. Coaches in this mindset soon start telling me that they have a feeling that they're "hiding out."

Hiding out? No . . . not a good activity. What if the airline pilot we were talking about did that? The flight attendant running down the aisle asking everyone, "Have you seen our pilot?" Not a situation you hope for if you're a passenger.

The lack of enthusiasm that leads to hiding out soon leads to all kinds of problems like procrastination, poor business decisions, low productivity and all the dysfunctions that come with not being able to create what you want.

So how about we just set that whole depressing cycle aside and do this profession like any other? We'll just do blue-collar work, maybe carry a notebook everywhere, learn the mechanics of the profession and have fun whacking away at it.

Maybe we can even be okay working from *inside* our comfort zone, doing what's *doable*, and being happy with having a very enjoyable, average day.

From there you can serve a lot of people well. It works for me and all the successful success coaches I know and work with. There's a quiet power inside that approach.

And it's from that relaxed, enjoyable, doable experience of my workday that the most creative ideas arise.

Some people create with words or with music or with a brush and paints. I like to make something beautiful when I run. I like to make people stop and say, "I've never seen anyone run like that before." It's more than just a race, it's a style. It's doing something better than anyone else. It's being creative.

~ **Steve Prefontaine**

When to create the impossible

Okay, it's time we reversed course. I've ranted enough about the dysfunctional temptation of approaching your new profession as if it were an impossible dream. It's time to look at creativity from a larger viewpoint.

My good friend Michael Neill is an author whose books you'll not only find in the *Recommended* section at the end of this book but also on my top bookshelf in my office, the one I reserve for books I want to read again and again.

Michael and I have taught courses together, and one of the most fun and interesting of these was a course on creative writing. His experience of creativity mirrors what mine has been. He sees that it's not a special gift given to the lucky, talented few; it's here for all of us in infinite supply. It's the energy that runs through everything and we not only "have" it, we are made up of it.

The fact that Michael and I seem to think alike can cause a problem for me. Especially when I fall out of my spacious spiritual place and get sucked into the tiny finger puppet known as my ego. Like when I started writing my first notes for this book and learned that Michael Neill's newest book was coming out and that it was called *Creating the Impossible*.

"Oh no," I thought (as I immediately *compared* myself to

him). "Not only will he say what I want to say better than I will, but judging by his title his book might even be one of those big-dream, pep-rally affairs that my book is going to come out against."

Well, the first fear was justified.

I read his book and saw how deeply and eloquently he wrote about the spiritual principles behind creativity. He describes those principles in ways I can only envy. But I'll get over the envy and the psychological misstep known as *comparing* soon enough.

My second fear was not justified. He does not evangelically advocate the same kind of super-achievement dream-questing that some popular motivators of new coaches do.

His book merely points out that when we're unaware of the depth of universal creativity, we can vastly underestimate what we can do in the world. We then take an unnecessarily gloomy (because it's contracted) view of who we are, which leads to even less of an appetite for life. When we are unaware of the spiritual principles that are always ready to lift us up with bright new ideas it almost feels like we're losing our vision. We no longer see possibilities. Most of the fun things we always wanted to do now look "impossible."

Michael's book inspires us to take a second look at the impossible—and then to brush away the cobwebby thought-clusters that are in the way of seeing potential creation.

Read his book and perhaps you'll wake up to the spiritual principles that feed us creatively. It could happen! (And waking up can happen in a million other ways if you're open. The painter Paul Cézanne said, "The day is coming when a single carrot, freshly observed, will set off a revolution.")

I was happy to see that Michael's book begins with a story I'd heard him tell before. It was a story about some poor guy who raised his hand at a talk Michael was giving about these unlimited principles. The guy said okay, but what about the *limits* of human creativity?

Always gracious, Michael allowed that an individual person's creative output would of course be limited, but the *source* of that creativity was unlimited. It went on to be a good, long, clear, respectful answer punctuated at the end by Michael smiling, shrugging and then finishing after a long pause by saying, "You are the infinite creative potential of the entire f**king universe—deal with it."

Michael's sixteen-year-old daughter was sitting in the back of the room on her phone when Michael said that, and she then tweeted his final quote out, followed simply by "#MyDad."

I've asked Michael to repeat this little story more than once when I'm on group calls with him, not only because it's funny, but also because it says so much. I mean it's just one sentence, but if someone could really hear it and get it and see the truth of it, they might experience a full-on reversal of their worldview right then and there. In those few words!

That's why I take the time to tell about it. Not only so you'll read his book and be guided by it to create for yourself what previously looked impossible to you, but also so that you'll maybe dance awhile with the wisdom of that quote.

Give it a second look.

He said, "You *are* the infinite, creative potential of the entire f**king universe." Notice that he said "you are" it. He didn't say you "have access to it," to that creative potential.

Many spiritual teachers tell you that you are "connected to" or "have access to" spirit, as if you are a thing that's here, and spirit is a different thing that's out there. They seem to stress the separation. Some say spirit "has your back," like it's a good and loyal (but very separate) gang member.

If Michael had said that that man "had access to" infinite

creative potential it would be heard and understood differently. He might see infinite creativity as something that was over *there* somewhere in a container. Maybe he'd picture it as something in a magic lamp, the future object of a vision quest or a hero's journey. While he himself was over *here* trying to survive as a skin-encapsulated ego.

Just a lonely guy wishing he were more creative.

That's the problem with trying to find *access*. Even when you think you've found it, it could end up like bad Wi-Fi. It doesn't connect you like you hoped it would. Because when it comes to creativity you'll be trying to connect to what you already are.

It would be like the Internet itself asking you for Wi-F.

You'd ask the Internet, "Why do you want Wi-F?"

"To connect to the Internet."

"But you already are the Internet."

The dream merchants who market and peddle *access* are usually as innocent and clueless about it as their customers. They think they can sell you access to creativity and you buy it because you think it's gotta be out there somewhere and maybe it's with those merchants. But it is not.

So selling access to it will never deliver it.

Let's look now at how the quote ends. After he informs (reveals? reminds?) his audience member that he, the questioner himself, is the infinite creative potential of the entire universe, Michael tells him to "deal with it."

You might be thinking that "deal with it" is just a tossed-off street phrase. As in, "Okay, Dude, just deal with it."

But I like to see it as more than dismissive. I like to see it as a strong prescription. Much stronger than, "Think about it," which would be asking the questioner to file it away in his thought cloud.

An insight into infinite creativity won't be of any use to him if it gets put into that thought cloud along with all the other swirls of advice, opinions, critiques, slogans, mantras, beliefs, memories, mentations, regrets, platitudes and aphorisms that circle there forever like aimless hordes of flimsy buzzards looking to someday feed on an abandoned seeker's heart.

How could that help a person understand creativity?

No. No more *thinking* about it. "Deal with it" is the prescription.

Because when you deal with something, you have to engage with it. Now you know you have to dance with it. And then, sooner or later, when the dance has slowed down somewhere toward the end of the music, you can hold it if it lets you, and embrace it if it lets you.

I think about Michael's talk and sometimes wonder what became of the questioner. Did he dance with infinite creativity? And if he did, what kind of music might have been playing? Oh, here, maybe this is it; it's Leonard Cohen singing his haunting song, "Dance Me to The End of Love."

> Dance me to your beauty
> with a burning violin
> Dance me through the panic
> till I'm gathered safely in
>
> ~ Leonard Cohen

When you look at an object, turn your head and see the source of looking. Be aware that you are the light of all perception.

~ Jean Klein

Who have you created?

My work in the world of corporate training took off when I created a course that taught employees various thinking tools that were designed to inspire them to take personal responsibility for their own spirit and morale.

Obviously companies liked that training because anything that improved morale ultimately benefitted productivity, performance and the bottom line. When people are upbeat they are more innovative, more collaborative and more energetic.

What companies didn't know was that what inspired me to create the course was my own study of the work of the spiritual teachers Alan Watts, Yogananda and Krishnamurti, and the philosophy of Colin Wilson. Reading and listening to their works deepened a "spiritual awakening" that occurred for me during my recovery from alcoholism (about which I've written more extensively in my cheerfully-titled book, *Death Wish*).

The corporate course I taught was about the power we have to create who we are—at least at the social level, where we create what we call "personality." I talked about creating how you're going to show up in the world. I talked about Shakespeare's stage.

Shakespeare's character Jacques in *As You Like It* says,

"All the world's a stage,

And all the men and women merely players;

They have their exits and their entrances . . ."

If they didn't resonate with Shakespeare, I'd remind them of Elvis Presley's hit song "Are You Lonesome Tonight." It has a spoken part in the middle of the song that begins with Elvis saying, "Someone said the world's a stage, and you must play a part . . ."

So the idea has been out there!

We are all playing a part. Which means there is nothing inevitable or permanent about "who we are being." Remember when you were little kids at play and yelling out, "I'll be Batman, you're Robin!"

Most people would agree that when we're in community theater or at a Halloween party we play parts. They'd even concede that they've done some serious play-acting pretending to be themselves when they're trying to impress someone or get something. I remember doing a great impression of a grateful, sincere, apologetic boy while being scolded and disciplined by my father or a schoolteacher.

People relate to and accept that kind of play-acting. But they also assume that they're just putting that act *on top of* who they really are. The real, true personality—who they think they are when they think they're being "authentic."

And the people who took my courses would usually take it on that level. They learned new ways of being like they were acting "as if." So they learned the benefits of acting and speaking "as if" they were owners of their own spirit and morale instead of victims of other people and circumstances. It worked for them. They felt better. They got along with people better. And by communicating in ways that took more responsibility for their own lives and happiness, they were able to see better relationships emerge in the work place.

They also learned, in those courses, about the research work of positive psychology and especially the books on optimism by Dr. Martin Seligman, who has demonstrated that optimism and pessimism are not permanent personality characteristics. Optimism was proven to be a skill that could be developed over time with practice and study and insight.

Sharing the news of that research sealed the deal. People in my courses couldn't argue with it. It wasn't just a theory. So they became excited about changing themselves for the better. They were able to see that the changes would be a benefit to them personally and not just some new training the company wanted them to take to benefit the company's bottom line.

Excited by the widespread success of that training, I wrote a book version of the course, and I called it *Reinventing Yourself*. The book went on to become a bestseller and just recently the publisher put out a "20th Anniversary" revised edition that for some reason left out the book's most important quote:

Why are you unhappy?
Because 99.9 percent
Of everything you think
And of everything you do,
Is for yourself—
And there isn't one.

~ Wu Wei Wu

That quote, when I first saw it, almost knocked me over. It expressed my own deep spiritual realization (for lack of a better term) that happened during addiction recovery. The wakeup call went something like this: As far as who you are, it's all a creation. Even your seemingly "authentic" personality, the one you think you're improving or adding play-acting on top of—that first personality, the real you, was just made up.

Talk about basic creativity!

Now I don't mean that at the level of spirit and soul, at the level of God-given awareness and *being*, some individual human called me created that. I'm referring to what Alan Watts called our "skin-encapsulated ego." That ego with a birth certificate with a random name on it (a name some partially drunk parent might have chuckled about)—that's what I'm referring to. That's made up.

We make the permanence of that person's identity up. Then we believe our own story about ourselves. And that story, like any lie repeated enough times or believed deeply enough, sooner or later feels really true. No question. Right down to the depths of our understanding of the word "true."

You see this guy? This guy's in love with his story. Pull the string coming out of his back and he'll say, "This is what I'm like."

This kind of capacity the brain has to believe stories that are not true is how and why certain people who are "skilled" at this can beat lie detector tests. To them, what they are saying is not a lie.

That's how they beat the test.

But here's the problem with talking or writing about this kind of spiritual awakening or neurological insight: people will think you are crazytown.

So in my course I had to make a concession to that, to the prevailing beliefs of the culture and society that we are all permanent, disconnected, individual personalities with permanent traits and characteristics. I had to have it be okay with me that most people thought they were only learning to be more creative about how they showed up in the world to their families and co-workers and leaders. I rationalized it by thinking it would be a good start. And in a sense, it really was, so I have no regrets.

Deep down I wanted them to get it at a more spiritual level. Sometimes I even said things in front of the room like, ". . . and one of the reasons you *have* this ability to reinvent yourself is that you invented yourself to begin with. You just didn't realize it."

Hmmm . . . Puzzled looks. Sometimes occasional smiles. But never mind you guys, back to work, on to strategies and communication systems! Self-improvement!

I'm not assuming you'll take my word for any of this "you are made up" stuff being true. I mean, it can't be true yet if it's not true for you. I'm just taking the risk of relating my own experience with it and justifying that by pointing out how it has influenced my understanding of the nature and power of creativity.

There are wiser and braver people than I am who write and teach exclusively about this kind of spiritual awakening and my favorite and most helpful people who do that are listed in the back of the book in the *Recommended* section. I urge you to read them and discover for yourself how exciting and real the awakenings can be.

I certainly don't recommend the path I took. There was blind luck that had to occur. Even for me to be alive today. The path took me from bottomed-out alcoholism and addiction, bankruptcy and divorce into a program of spiritual recovery. The realization that I was not just my ego gave me the strange and beautiful feeling that the mystic Catholic philosopher G.K. Chesterton called "absurd good news."

Part of that good news is that no matter what level you look at this, from a game-of-life practical level all the way up to crazytown spiritual, this much is true: you get to create who you want to be, on this playing field, in this game of life, and there isn't anyone out there who can stop you.

If we are going to insist on identifying with just the little self in here, then others are going to bruise it, insult it, injure it. The ego, then, is kept in existence by a collection of emotional insults; it carries its personal bruises as the fabric of its very existence. It actively collects hurts and insults, even while resenting them, because without its bruises it would be, literally, nothing.

~ **Ken Wilber**

Conversation becomes co-creation

My professional life these days consists of conversations. People call me, or visit me, and we talk.

Someone once asked Steve Hardison just how this coaching thing would work. They expected to hear an answer filled with complexity and depth, but what Steve said was, "You talk and I listen. Then I talk and you listen."

That's the process, for sure. And I admired Steve for giving the answer Lao-Tse might have given. But he (knowingly) left out the best part of what really happens. He had to leave it out because words don't reach it. He left out what gets created.

What gets created is an insightful breakthrough that has us see life differently and then live life differently. This breakthrough arises in the field of creative listening.

When you drop out of the equation and can now listen openly to a person from a wide-open place beyond personal concerns and judgments of them, from beyond the ego, then real understanding shows up. And with more understanding, more compassion.

Soon you're seeing ways to create a relationship based on this wide-open listening. Inspired ideas. They always come from beyond. Beyond the thought-bound ego. Beyond the personal.

The ego never creates anything.

Its job is to worry about lack of creation . . . and to find out how to personalize that lack. So it has a heartless job, the performance of which does us no good whatsoever.

But my own experience is that creativity comes from beyond the ego, even if the ego is what told me to sit down to solve something. Creativity itself comes from beyond the ego, or the contracted "me" made up of personal thoughts, psychic wounds, fears and desperate desires.

So I want to allow all of that to drop out when I'm listening. I want my agenda to disappear.

I've learned a great deal about listening in the past year through my work with Dr. Mark Howard, a psychologist who assisted me in understanding how clients can receive the greatest benefits from a coaching conversation.

The new practice for me was learning to listen without myself being in the picture. So if I took a photo of you and me in our session when we looked at the picture later I wouldn't be in it. Ideally.

You can't photograph true listening.

And without the ego there to obstruct everything, creative impulses, little flashes of light, appear. They appear because they don't have to work their way through the thought-cluster of fear-based judgments.

They just appear.

Maybe that's why when I heard my children playing with other children (when they were young and had under-developed egos) I'd so often hear them yell out excitedly, "Hey! I've got an idea!"

I've spent many hours inside companies and other organizations and I've never heard an adult yell that out.

Listening is a magnetic and strange thing, a creative force. The friends who listen to us are the ones we move toward. When we are listened to, it creates us, makes us unfold and expand.

~ Karl A. Menninger

Someone set me free

For many years my job was songwriter. I co-wrote songs with my brilliant collaborator Fred Knipe. One of my favorite songs we wrote was called "The Middle of Nowhere." One line was, "Out there in the middle of nowhere, someone set me free."

Normally the idea of being "in the middle of nowhere" is not so good. But something about that phrase was haunting. And it's funny what happens when you take a second look at a phrase like that. Even funnier when you put music to it. It changes. What seems bleak and hopeless changes into something else.

Just like a person's life when you add the awareness of eternal creativity to it. It's like putting music to words that never would have been heard.

Writing that song got a small premonition of insight started in me back then. The insight that opens more every time I hear my recording of Fred singing it. What I now see is that there's *freedom* in the middle of nowhere.

In my mind, the middle of nowhere is where creativity seems to live when we don't know we have it. It's as if we're in the eye of the storm, in the middle of a hurricane of creative energy. It's where I drop my preconceived thoughts and beliefs about who I am. Or even what I should do next.

From here, I can open to the source of spirit as taught by Dr. Ron Hulnick in his courses on spiritual psychology. He often invited his students to be willing to enter and stay awhile in "the divine unknowing," a place the ego always wants to avoid, but a place where you will feel your true creative power.

Ever since happiness heard your name,
it has been running through the streets
trying to find you.

~ **Hafez**

The space where it happens

Now let's bring this metaphor back to earth. Down here in the material world of achievement and making a living I have found another synchronicity for the middle of nowhere.

And you'll like this, because it's practical and it helps you get what you want. It also helps you build new, real-world skills that you may never have tried before.

It's that middle part.

That, too, connects to your creativity, because that's where the expression best happens. Right there in the middle.

My experience in my own life and in the decades I've spent helping clients create what they want makes me almost ready to say that *all* progress takes place in what we're going to call the middle.

The middle ground! The space between the polarities. The space between the extremes. The open, green and grassy playing field between the cast-iron goal posts. Where all progress plays out.

Most people *not* making good progress are stuck because they're not in that place. That middle ground. Instead, they have gone to extremes. They've gotten hooked on a habit of jumping to extreme polarities of judgments of themselves.

They don't see the power of the middle.

The most common polarities people get magnetized to are **I'm bad at this** way over on one extreme, and **I'm good at this** on the other end. Their activities and attempts at practicing a skill don't last long because the first sign of not being good at it pulls them back to the bad pole. It's like the force of a huge magnet. They're constantly stuck on one pole or the other.

"I tried doing some of that videoconferencing with my team managers," a client I'll call Jennie told me. "It's just not my thing. I'm not good at it. I have to be honest with you—and with myself."

She wanted me to help her look for other ways to communicate with and effectively lead her team at work.

I had been noticing that in Jennie's world her potential for creative expression was often cut short by the polar opposites her mind is drawn to all day. Her thoughts were like monkeys who swung between, "I'm good at this" and "I'm bad at that." Her potential for progress was frozen by the judgments that made up her polar opposites.

She might have stayed that way forever if she hadn't become willing to explore the field of play known as the middle.

In the middle you don't care about whether you're good or bad. And that's the key to the power of the middle.

You're just jumping into action and communication and moving right along, happy to see tiny improvements, sometimes even molecular in size, and happy to be out there on the field, learning as you go, not bad, not good, but certainly getting better.

Soon people try to guess at why you get better and better while other people quit. Those who drop out of the game you keep improving at will try to assign a permanent characteristic to your personality, a quality they don't have. And because they live in a world of permanent things with permanent people in it, finding a label to put on you makes sense to them. They label everything.

But that's not the world you are living in, and even flourishing in, now that you've found the middle.

Now your world is the *real* world—full of creative energy and movement—and you are progressing so nicely because you've moved off your polar opposites and into the middle. Now you're starting to learn, from your experience in the middle, that creativity thrives there. It flourishes in a land without judgment. It expands in a space without pressure.

When Jennie had tried to facilitate her team conference she immediately "found out" she wasn't good at it. Being on video made her a little self-conscious. She fumbled around with muting and unmuting the team members when they wanted to talk. So she knew right away which polar opposite this activity belonged to. She felt the pull. She was **bad at this**. She was ready to put that label on it and quit.

"Not if you want to work with me," I told her.

She asked me what I meant.

I told her that if she was going to work with me, we weren't going to honor the extreme polar opposites of judgment. Because they aren't real. They don't match up with how the world works. They don't acknowledge the flow of energy moving at all times and the creativity it makes available.

Polarization tries to stop the ever-changing dance of life. It tries to freeze it over on one end so it can label it.

You claim to be bad at doing something and that freezes you there.

But are you're "bad" at doing that? Compared to what? Compared to how you were last week? Compared to then, you're not bad at all!

Maybe you've found someone, someone you can name for me that you can compare yourself unfavorably to, and that will put you at your polar extreme of "bad." But why? What if there will always be someone you can find who does it better and always someone you can find who does it worse? What does that matter? What does that tell us? Nothing real. Nothing useful.

The addiction to polar opposites leads to a life of comparing which leads to a life of extreme self-judgment based on randomness. You'll be passing your time jumping to gratuitous conclusions and finding yourself frozen into the opposites you've chosen.

You could do that forever.

Or you could see what it's like out here in the middle of the field. Out here between bad and good, between rejected and accepted, between the minors and the majors, is the land of real-world progress where your God-given creativity has a chance to get expressed every day. This is the freedom of the middle. You are free here to work and play without restraint. You're not good at what you do here, or bad at what you do. You're just having fun and making progress.

Over time Jennie saw the value in taking the field again. She learned to enjoy the imperfect middle . . . the life force itself. She focused on serving her people with conferences and getting a little better at it each time. Today Jennie uses videoconferencing two or three times a week as if it were just a natural and easy expression of her creativity. It no longer occurs to her to try to find out whether she's bad or good at it, or if it's the right fit for her permanent personality. Her recent promotion came with the requirement that she be willing to set up and lead teleconference meetings internationally so they could include teams in other parts of the world.

When she was asked during her promotion interview if she'd be willing to handle that she said of course she would. That wouldn't be a problem at all. In fact, she was looking forward to it.

You may be tempted to point out to me by now that there really isn't a lot of skill involved in learning to host a videoconference. And that you yourself do some version of that all the time. I get that, but that's *why* I wanted to use Jennie's experience for an example. If I used someone who learned to write complicated code or play the cello in a symphony orchestra it would miss the point. (Even though the middle works the same way for those people too.)

The missed point would have been that creativity is cued up and ready to play anywhere and everywhere. No occasion is too small. It's there for you in every moment.

And moving out of the polar extremes caused by self-judgment will give you a middle field of play you never knew you had. Once you get there you'll be focused and present to the now. You won't be nervously looking over your shoulder to see if a judgment is coming to get you. The outer world of distractions won't undermine you now that you're creating from here.

Welcome to the middle of nowhere.

Soon to be seen as the middle of everywhere.

All we are is peace, love, and wisdom, and the power to create the illusion that we are not.

~ Jack Pransky

God bless the child

People have always marveled at how unafraid children are to express their creativity. I remember this with my own children, and now with my grandchildren I see it even more clearly that they don't think they're bad at *anything*.

They're surprised when you object to how their crayons have colored the wall in your dining room. They don't understand why you don't enjoy it when they come pound the high-end keys on the piano while you're trying to play a lovely, soft song like "The Middle of Nowhere."

Picasso said, "All children are artists; the trick is to remain an artist."

My musical friend and song co-writer Fred used to help me relax into the middle ground whenever I was stuck and felt I couldn't create. One time I called him in desperation. I was impaled on one of the polar opposites ("I'm not good at this!") and he said something I'll never forget.

"Just be Stevie."

Stevie was my little grandson at the time. He was always so happy and playful, making up games and stories with his tiny action figures.

I asked Fred what he meant. He said, "Just play with it like he would do. And play just to play, not as a means to an end. Play with no purpose."

By picturing my little grandson I was able to jump into the project I was working on right away.

Fred and I have since then talked about Picasso's observation that all children are artists. I know now it's because they haven't been polarized yet. There are no categories they know to put themselves in. No self-judgment.

Welcome to life in the middle. It's so clear to me when I'm watching children that there's freedom there.

Fred wrote a song about this, the lyrics for which I've included as the last words (and music) in this book. It's about you "In Your Right Mind," when you're childishly wild and free to create.

To create one must be willing to be stone
   stupid,
to sit upon a throne on top of a jackass
and spill rubies from one's mouth.

~ Clarissa Pinkola Estés

It's more than making things

Not all creating involves making something. Even though we usually think of it that way. We think things like, "What's the next *thing* I want to create?"

That question is almost always asking what one should produce, or manufacture, or string together so it can be added to a world that didn't have it before.

So we think of creating a new blog, or a sand castle on the beach, or a big meal with experimental recipes or a quilt or a painting or a new business or a rap musical based on the life of one of the founding fathers. Things created that weren't here before. Things added to life.

But creativity is more versatile and powerful than just that.

Because it can take away as well as add.

When I remove clutter from my room and clean the desk and windows I have *created* a freshly re-organized and clean workspace. When I take books and clothing and furniture to the Salvation Army I've *created* space in the home for a better life.

And if I realized I was *creating* during those activities I'd be having a much better time. Instead, I often fall victim to the culture's story that those activities are dull and tedious. Not available for enjoyment. No joy to be taken from something you have to get *through*.

Michelangelo notwithstanding. (Michelangelo created beautiful statues by carving away and taking away marble from a large slab of stone.)

Ralph Waldo Emerson said, "As the gardener, by severe pruning, forces the sap of the tree into one or two vigorous limbs, so should you stop off your miscellaneous activity and concentrate your force on one or a few points."

Why should you do that?

Because more creative light and power is now available for the few points really important to you! So the pruning is a great idea. Look at the dying branches the gardener took away from the tree. Doesn't the tree look healthier and more beautiful?

When you creatively prune your office desk does it not appear to be more clean and beautiful? And the stuff you hauled out of the house to Salvation Army—didn't it open up and beautify your home? You are creating beauty.

We don't glamorize severe pruning. We don't even want to talk much about it. Even though upon further review it's seen to be profoundly creative. So is organizing and cleaning. By doing those creative activities we produce new beauty.

Hall of Fame basketball star Kobe Bryant tells young college players that the path to success in sports lies in being willing to "edit your life!" By *editing* he means to delete and remove all the short-term temptations and distractions pulling you away from your long-term objective—the career you want to create. Editing is his word for pruning.

After two years of working on "Hallelujah," Leonard Cohen still had an unfinished song that had eighty trial verses. Now it was time for the real creativity: editing and pruning.

My friend Dusan Djukich is a consultant who helps small

business owners create more productive businesses. When he sits down with a new client to review the current problematic state of their life and business he asks an important question:

"What are you tolerating?"

In that moment, Dusan is his own version of Michelangelo. He's looking for what problematic thing can be cut away from his client's cluttered life. They will work together to edit and prune those things out of existence. That will create the life the client wants.

Most of us miss out on using this vital form of creativity by labeling it incorrectly. It's not drudgery until we say it is. Pruning, editing and deleting are acts of creativity that we can look forward to with as much good feeling as we get when we're "making something."

Average people like you and I can thrill to subtracting as much as we do to adding. We can start doing this ourselves, no matter how "not creative" we think we are. We don't have to leave all this subtractive power in the hands of Michelangelo and Dusan Djukich. We don't have to believe that they have "access" to powers we don't have access to. They don't.

Society has a condescending view of this form of creative expression because of its narrow belief of what is creative. It has blinders to creativity. There aren't great media tributes to people whose very job titles have become terms of disparagement, like "cleaning ladies," "garbage men" or "exterminators." They just take stuff away!

We don't see that they create beauty by what they know to take away. But when we do, it can open many aspects of our own lives to acts of creativity.

The great artists like Michelangelo and Blake and Tolstoy—like Christ whom Blake called an artist because he had one of the most creative imaginations that ever was on earth—do not want security, egoistic or materialistic. Why, it never occurs to them.

~ Brenda Ueland

I can always just breathe in

If people create best when they are inspired, then I want to breathe in, which is what inspiration actually means, and feel how inspired I feel when I hear a song whose lyrics delight me, like Leonard Cohen's when he sings (or Judy Collins sings or Roberta Flack sings) his song, "Hey, That's No Way to Say Goodbye":

> I loved you in the morning,
> our kisses deep and warm
> Your hair upon the pillow,
> like a sleepy golden storm

As I'm breathing in the first two lines of that song, I want to read them again. And then listen to them again.

But were you to ask me to carefully analyze why or how the song delights me (because maybe you want to be able to write like that, and so you want to understand the underlying process behind it) my words would just be, after a long silence, "Your hair upon the pillow, like a sleepy golden storm."

Because what else could I say?

Fortunately for me, as I look to inspiration to wake me up to the creativity I already am, I *can* find something else to say to your question about that song lyric, and where the poetry might come from. The clue would be from Cohen himself in his novel *Beautiful Losers*. Because in there I find this: "God is alive. Magic is afoot."

I'm not following you.

Okay, I'm saying maybe that's *how* he wrote it. You're looking for a "how," right? A process to learn? What if his process was simply knowing that "God is alive. Magic is afoot."

Can you say more about that?

Cohen can say more about that, not I. In the book he goes on. After he writes "God is alive. Magic is afoot." He follows it with, "Alive is afoot. Magic never died."

Oh.

He goes on like that. It's spellbinding actually. He goes on and on. Read the full chapter, the full passage. You can find it online. You can read it to yourself as an incantation. Buffy Sainte Marie turned it into a song, a strange, native-people's mystical drone of a song. A spell. It will take you places. Leave you spellbound. The whole passage is the closest thing I've ever seen to a poetic confirmation of creativity's source. And such an inspiration:

> God is alive; Magic is afoot
> God is afoot; Magic is alive
> Alive is afoot . . . Magic never died . . .
> This I mean to whisper to my mind
> This I mean to laugh with in my mind
>
> This I mean my mind to serve 'til
> Service is but Magic, moving through the world
> And mind itself is Magic coursing through the flesh
> And flesh itself is Magic dancing on a clock
> And time itself, the Magic length of God

> ~ Leonard Cohen

Is this the kind of inspiration you have to get hooked by before you before you create something?

No. It's not a requirement. I used to think it was—that you have to be inspired in order to create. But that turns out to be untrue. You can create any time. And why would that be? I'm just guessing it's because whether you're feeling inspired or not, God is alive and magic is always afoot.

So you don't *need* inspiration to begin creating what you want to create. You can just get to work. But that doesn't mean you can't also be a big fan of inspiration and enjoy finding it.

I'm inspired by acts of creation that are amazingly beautiful and moving. And I keep noticing that they are timeless. They don't have to be trendy or up to date. Brenda Ueland's inspiring book was written in 1938, and the poet who most inspired *her*, William Blake, was born in 1757! He famously wrote:

To see a World in a Grain of Sand
And a Heaven in a Wild Flower,
Hold *Infinity* in the palm of your hand
And Eternity in an hour.

Wow. And if I can risk being crude in the face of such beautiful writing, he nails it. Right there. That's what it is to fully know you are Creator. It's to see what the poem sees and to hold what the poet holds . . . to hold infinity in the palm of your hand and eternity in an hour. That's it. He knew. He saw.

Magic is afoot
It cannot come to harm
It rests in an empty palm
It spawns in an empty mind
But Magic is no instrument
Magic is the end.

~ Leonard Cohen

In Your Right Mind

Words & Music by Fred Knipe

All little kids are artists
And their materials are always at hand
For them everywhere's a good place to get started
In the dirt...in the street...in the sand

But this is too wise to call innocence
When we spend our lives
Straining our eyes
And they, when they want, see magnificence
In the dirt, in the street, in the grass, in the weeds
In the concrete, the cardboard, the glass
On the beach, on the sidewalk, in trash
In the clouds in the ditch in the bath in the mud
In light and in shadow
In the ashes
Or the wood

Who in their right mind
Would stop at the moment
When cities are rising out of sticks and sand?
Who would swallow their words
just when words become stories?
Swallow their sound as it turns into song

Not you in your right mind
You can choose to go with it
To fill the idea
To love it and warm it
A child in your right mind
You trust your own beauty
And you're never foolish
You're never wrong

Recommended

Reading

Remembering the Light Within by Drs. Ron and Mary Hulnick

The Path of No Resistance by Garret Kramer

The Relationship Handbook by George S. Pransky, Ph.D.

Loving What Is by Byron Katie

Why Materialism Is Baloney by Bernardo Kastrup

Creating the Impossible by Michael Neill

The Direct Path by Greg Goode

The Nature of Consciousness by Rupert Spira

Eternity Now by Francis Lucille

Deep Work by Cal Newport

Coming Home by Dicken Bettinger and Natasha Swerdloff

Listening

9Ninety9 by Fred Knipe

And the two songs mentioned in this book by Fred Knipe "Middle of Nowhere" and "In Your Right Mind" available on www.Imindshift.com

I See Black Light by Lacy Wilder

Viewing

YouTube videos by:

Francis Lucille
Rupert Spira
Bernardo Kastrup
Dr. Mark Howard
Dicken Bettinger

About the author

Steve Chandler has written dozens of books on subjects that swing dizzyingly from Jane Austen to baseball to business coaching to travel to obituaries to Moby Dick. He is the author of the bestsellers *Crazy Good* and *Time Warrior*.

He lives in Birmingham, Michigan, with his wife and editor, Kathy, and two hell hounds.

You may find him and learn of his latest adventures at www.stevechandler.com.

Books by Steve Chandler

RIGHT NOW
Death Wish
Crazy Good
37 Ways to BOOST Your Coaching Practice
Wealth Warrior
Time Warrior
The Life Coaching Connection
Fearless
The Woman Who Attracted Money
Shift Your Mind Shift the World
17 Lies That Are Holding You Back
10 Commitments to Your Success
Reinventing Yourself
The Story of You
100 Ways to Motivate Yourself
How to Get Clients
50 Ways to Create Great Relationships
The Joy of Selling
Powerful Graceful Success
RelationShift (with Michael Bassoff)
The Small Business Millionaire (with Sam Beckford)
100 Ways to Create Wealth (with Sam Beckford)
9 Lies That Are Holding Your Business Back
(with Sam Beckford)
Business Coaching (with Sam Beckford)
100 Ways to Motivate Others (with Scott Richardson)
The Hands Off Manager (with Duane Black)
Two Guys On the Road (with Terrence Hill)
Two Guys Read the Box Scores (with Terrence Hill)
Two Guys Read Jane Austen (with Terrence Hill)

Two Guys Read Moby Dick (with Terrence Hill)
Two Guys Read the Obituaries (with Terrence Hill)
The Prosperous Coach (with Rich Litvin)

Audio by Steve Chandler

9 Lies That Are Holding Your Business Back
10 Habits of Successful Salespeople
17 Sales Lies
37 Ways to BOOST Your Coaching Practice (audiobook)
Are You A Doer Or A Feeler?
Challenges
Choosing
Crazy Good (audiobook)
Creating Clients: Referrals
Creating Clients: The 18 Disciplines
Creative Relationships
Death Wish (audiobook)
Expectation vs. Agreement
Fearless (audiobook)
Financially Fearless
How To Double Your Income As A Coach
How to Get Clients (audiobook)
How To Help A Pessimist
How To Solve Problems
Information vs. Transformation
Is It A Dream Or A Project?
Making A Difference
MindShift: The Steve Chandler Success Course
Ownership And Leadership
People People
Personality Reinvented
Purpose vs. Personality
Serving vs. Pleasing People
Testing vs. Trusting
The Creating Wealth audio series

The Fearless Mindset
The Focused Leader
The Function Of Optimism
The Joy Of Succeeding
The Owner / Victim Choice
The Prosperous Coach (audiobook)
The Ultimate Time Management System
Time Warrior (audiobook)
Wealth Warrior (audiobook)
Welcoming Every Circumstance
Who You Know vs. What You Do
Why Should I Reinvent Myself?
You'll Get What You Want By Asking For It

Publisher's Catalogue

The Prosperous Series

#1 The Prosperous Coach: Increase Income and Impact for You and Your Clients (Steve Chandler and Rich Litvin)

#2 The Prosperous Hip Hop Producer: My Beat-Making Journey from My Grandma's Patio to a Six-Figure Business (Curtiss King)

* * *

Devon Bandison

Fatherhood Is Leadership: Your Playbook for Success, Self-Leadership, and a Richer Life

Sir Fairfax L. Cartwright

The Mystic Rose from the Garden of the King

Steve Chandler

37 Ways to BOOST Your Coaching Practice: PLUS: the 17 Lies That Hold Coaches Back and the Truth That Sets Them Free

50 Ways to Create Great Relationships

Business Coaching (Steve Chandler and Sam Beckford)

Crazy Good: A Book of CHOICES

CREATOR

Death Wish: The Path through Addiction to a Glorious Life

Fearless: Creating the Courage to Change the Things You Can

RIGHT NOW: Mastering the Beauty of the Present Moment

The Prosperous Coach: Increase Income and Impact for You and Your Clients (The Prosperous Series #1) (Steve Chandler and Rich Litvin)

Shift Your Mind Shift The World (Revised Edition)

Time Warrior: How to defeat procrastination, people-pleasing, self-doubt, over-commitment, broken promises and chaos

Wealth Warrior: The Personal Prosperity Revolution

Kazimierz Dąbrowski

Positive Disintegration

The Philosophy of Essence: A Developmental Philosophy Based on the Theory of Positive Disintegration

Charles Dickens

A Christmas Carol: A Special Full-Color, Fully-Illustrated Edition

James F. Gesualdi

Excellence Beyond Compliance: Enhancing Animal Welfare Through the Constructive Use of the Animal Welfare Act

Janice Goldman

Let's Talk About Money: The Girlfriends' Guide to Protecting Her ASSets

Sylvia Hall

This Is Real Life: Love Notes to Wake You Up

Christy Harden

Guided by Your Own Stars: Connect with the Inner Voice and Discover Your Dreams

I Heart Raw: Reconnection and Rejuvenation Through the Transformative Power of Raw Foods

Curtiss King

The Prosperous Hip Hop Producer: My Beat-Making Journey from My Grandma's Patio to a Six-Figure Business (The Prosperous Series #2)

David Lindsay

A Blade for Sale: The Adventures of Monsieur de Mailly

Abraham H. Maslow

Personality and Growth: A Humanistic Psychologist in the Classroom

The Psychology of Science: A Reconnaissance

Being Abraham Maslow (DVD)

Maslow and Self-Actualization (DVD)

Albert Schweitzer

Reverence for Life: The Words of Albert Schweitzer

William Tillier

Personality Development Through Positive Disintegration: The Work of Kazimierz Dąbrowski

Margery Williams

The Velveteen Rabbit: or How Toys Become Real

Join our Mailing List:
www.MauriceBassett.com

MAURICE BASSETT
books for athletes of the mind